DEDICATION

This book is dedicated to you - the new college student.
We hope this book provides you with the tools and resources
that will allow you to make informed and educated decisions.
Decisions that will provide you with the academic,
personal, financial, and professional
success you deserve.

Life During College

Your Guide to Success

2nd Edition

A "Life After Graduation, LLC" Publication
5645 Kathryn Street • Alexandria, Virginia • 22303
(877) 569-9816 • www.LifeAfterGraduation.com

COPYRIGHT INFORMATION

2st Edition Copyrighted in April 2005

BOOK DISCLAIMER

The authors of this book and Life After Graduation, LLC have made their best efforts in preparing this book to be accurate and complete. The content of the book is not guaranteed to produce any particular results. In addition, the advice given in the book may not suit every individual's circumstances.

Therefore, the authors and Life After Graduation, LLC do not assume responsibility for advice given. As a result, each reader should consider their own circumstances and abilities and weigh them versus the advice given.

The authors and Life After Graduation, LLC are not in the business of rendering financial, legal, or any other professional advice. If any questions regarding legal or financial advice should arise, the reader should seek professional assistance.

The authors and Life After Graduation, LLC shall not be held liable for any damages arising from the book's content.

GETTING TO KNOW YOUR COLLEGE

ACHIEVING ACADEMIC SUCCESS

BECOMING A SUCCESSFUL STUDENT

LIVING ON YOUR OWN

As a college student, there will probably be no other time in your life when you will have so many resources available to you. From counseling and health care to security escorts and social events, there is a service to assist you with every aspect of your college career.

Unfortunately, many college students are unaware of just how many resources are available to them, and miss out on valuable, free and often fun opportunities simply because they don't take the time to become familiar with their college resources – and then use them. Don't let this happen to you!

This chapter will help you get the most out of the resources at your college by:

- Outlining the most common college resources.
- Offering tips on how best to use the resources available to you.

A list of resources available at most colleges follows.

Academic Advising – A more detailed explanation of academic advising is included in the Academic Advising chapter but, in general, academic advisors help students get the most out of their entire college experience. Academic advisors help students plan their schedules, choose their majors, map out a plan for graduation, and achieve their academic and post-graduation goals.

Alumni Association – Alumni associations are established to develop longterm relationships with students after they graduate. Alumni associations often offer members business networking and other career development opportunities, special discount programs, and invitations to social events.

Bookstore – While not free, bookstores offer students all of the textbooks and other materials they will need for their classes in one convenient location. Most college bookstores also offer used books at a reduced cost, and end-of-term book buy-back programs.

Bursar – Pronounced burr-sir, the bursur manages the financial records and needs of the college and will notify you about payments you owe to the college.

Campus Police – The goal of the campus police is to create an environment that keeps students safe as they learn, work, live and visit. In addition to the normal duties that police forces perform, services offered by campus police often include classes and publications on campus and personal safety, and security escorts for students traveling on campus after nightfall.

Career Services – The Career Services center or office may be the college resource that is most important to your future. Resources provided through career services include internship placements, resume development assistance, interviewing and networking support, career development classes and publications, job fairs, job boards, and career planning.

Computer/Information Technology (IT) Center – Most college students have their own computers, but many schools still offer students computer access on campus. This will come in handy on days when your personal computer crashes. Your IT center helps you establish your college e-mail account and may also offer computer classes and help on computer-related questions.

Counseling Center – College counseling centers offer students professional counseling help with both personal- and school-related problems. Your counseling center can be an invaluable resource at times when you need the most help during your college experience.

Dean of Students – The Dean of Students office is the liaison between students and the faculty and administration of the college, and helps to enhance the quality of campus life.

Disability Support Services – This office offers important support to students with all kinds of disabilities, including physical, mental and learning disabilities, and works to increase awareness and improve the quality of life for students with disabilities. Some services offered may include helping students with their course load, offering a support network for students with disabilities, exploring transportation, housing and academic accommodations options, as well as providing other opportunities to students with disabilities.

Financial Aid – The Financial Aid office works to eliminate the financial barriers that would otherwise discourage or prohibit college students from attending and completing college. This office employs experienced financial advisors who work with students to evaluate their financial needs and find the federal, state and/or scholarship financial assistance that help students fund their college education.

Greek Affairs – This office supports the educational and social goals of the fraternities and sororities on campus. Resources offered might include academic advising, membership recruitment, leadership development, community service, risk management and maintenance of the Greek system facilities.

Honors Program – Most colleges have an honors program that offers more challenging academics for advanced or gifted students. Access to this program is typically limited, but students accepted receive support to help them create a curriculum and campus life that is challenging and meets the students' needs.

International Student Services – This office serves as a home away from home for international students and can provide orientation services, advising and counseling, employment aid, health insurance programs, banking and financial services, immigration support, and resources for families of international students.

Library – Every college has a central library that students can use to conduct research, find recreational reading materials, or use as a quite place to study. Most colleges also have departmental libraries. These libraries carry a more extensive selection of materials related to the specific department's needs.

Multicultural Affairs – The office of multicultural affairs provides support to multicultural students to help them achieve their goals, and works to promote awareness, respect and acceptance of diversity and multiculturalism.

Ombudsman – An ombudsman is an advocate for students who mediates and resolves student conflicts and concerns. For example, if you believe a professor is treating you unfairly, an ombudsman can help you investigate your concerns, meet with relevant parties and reach a resolution.

Parent Services – College is a time of transition for new students, of course. But believe it or not, parents of college students also go through a period of adjustment. The Parent Services office works to minimize parent concerns, establish and maintain a strong relationship with parents, and keep parents informed about academic issues through ongoing communication.

Registrar – The registrar performs a range of student services, including course scheduling, fee waivers, residency and enrollment issues, transcripts, grade reporting, and billing.

Residence Life – This office primarily maintains campus housing and dining facilities, and may also develop programs and services such as meal plans, room assignments and roommate matching.

Student Activities Center – Student Activities centers plan and organize fun, social and educational activities and events both on and off campus for students. Guest speakers, sports leagues and travel – such as rock climbing or skiing trips – are all examples of activities this office may offer.

Student Health Center – Many colleges offer students access to some form of quality, affordable and accessible health care services, even if they do not have health insurance. Some colleges have a fully operational hospital, while others employ just a nurse practitioner. Immunizations, reduced-cost prescriptions through an on-campus pharmacy, diagnosis and treatment of common illnesses and minor injuries, and health education outreach are some of the common services provided by Student Health centers.

Student Legal Services – If you find yourself in need of legal help, your college may offer some form of free or reduced-cost legal services. Student legal services may also offer outreach and education on rights and other legal issues.

Student Recreation or Athletic Center – Many colleges now offer on-campus recreation or athletic centers where students and staff can participate in exercise classes and work out on a variety of equipment. These centers also may offer access to pools, sports courts and fields, athletic equipment, fitness evaluation, and training and nutrition services.

Tutoring Centers – During the course of their college careers, many students need help with class work and studying. That is where the tutoring center comes in. Tutoring centers help match students with tutors in specific areas of study. Often, tutors are employed by the tutoring center and are free to students, though some colleges may charge fees.

Take Advantage of What Your College Has to Offer

To be sure you don't miss out on any valuable opportunities:

Do:

- ***Keep in mind that your college may refer to the above resources by different names*** or house several resources in one department. Your college may not offer all of the above resources; on the other hand, it may offer resources not listed here.

- ***Find out what is available at your college by referring to your college catalog or Web site***, or by speaking with your academic advisor.
- ***Remember that knowing what resources are available to you at your college and using them can save you money and time***, and greatly enrich your college experience.

Don't:

- ***Think that if you are living off-campus or at home you are not eligible for campus and college resources.*** Contact your college to find out what services and facilities are accessible to you as an off-campus or commuting student.
- ***Feel like a charity case for using college resources*** – you're paying for them! A portion of every student's tuition goes to support the resources your college offers.
- ***Forget that some college resources continue to be available to you as a graduate of your college.*** Sometimes, for a small fee, alumni are invited to use the college career center, take advantage of college legal services, or join the college recreation or athletic center to work out.

As a new college student, there are a lot of things you need to know that you won't learn in class. What classes should you take in the first place? What kinds of prerequisites are there for the major you are considering? Which instructors and classes will best suit your interests, strengths and personality? Luckily, you don't have to figure out all of this on your own. That's what academic advisors are for.

Your college actually has instructors and staff who are trained and experienced in helping students just like you navigate the world of college from acceptance to graduation. They are called academic advisors, and can be a college student's best friend. In fact, your journey to graduation will be much smoother if you choose and use your academic advisor well.

This chapter will help you get the most out of your academic advisor by:

- Explaining the role of an academic advisor.
- Outlining your rights and options.
- Describing your responsibilities as an advisee.

The Role of the Academic Advisor

The role of an academic advisor is to help you reach graduation as smoothly as possible, and to ensure that you get the most out of your college experience. A good academic advisor will help you:

- ***Develop your class schedule.***
- ***Successfully navigate the class add/drop process.***

- ***Organize your classes*** so that you can fulfill your requirements and graduate in a reasonable amount of time.
- ***Develop into a well-rounded student*** by giving you guidance and information about campus activities that may interest you.
- ***Explore alternative classes and courses of study*** that you may not have considered.
- ***Stay informed*** about course changes, policy changes and graduation requirements.
- ***Find help*** if you are struggling with school, work, or even personal or relationship issues.
- ***Accomplish your college and career goals.***

Your Academic Advising Rights and Options

Your hard work up to now has earned you a place at college. Now, as a tuition-paying college student, you have also earned access to an academic advisor who will serve you well during your college years. This includes:

The Right To An Academic Advisor Who Meets Your Specific Needs
When choosing an academic advisor, be sure to consider the following criteria:

- ***Are the advisor's office hours convenient for you?***
- ***Does the advisor express interest and concern*** about your academic choices and make you feel good about the choices you make?
- ***Does the advisor ask you a lot of questions*** about your goals for college and after graduation?
- ***Is the advisor knowledgeable*** about your major, and does the advisor offer a lot of suggestions?
- ***Is the advisor easy to talk with?***
- ***Does the advisor intimidate you,*** make your feel uncomfortable, or steer you in a direction that does not fit your interests and goals?

The Option To Change Academic Advisors
While many colleges initially assign students an academic advisor, you do have the option to change advisors. Of course, if you are lucky enough to be comfortable with the advisor that is assigned to you, don't fix what isn't broken. However, it is very common for college students to change advisors, even a few times, especially as they choose or change majors and work to find an advisor who is experienced in their course of study. Some things to consider before changing advisors:

- ***Get a second opinion*** and some recommendations on which advisor might suit your needs. Ask a respected instructor or an older student in your major for suggestions.
- ***Meet with several advisors*** to discuss your academic situation and your goals. Take the time to think about each advisor's responses and recommendations.
- ***Make sure you understand the process of changing advisors*** and take the time to make the change correctly. Changing advisors improperly can delay your class registration or cause other problems.
- ***If your request to change advisors is denied for some reason, resolve the problem right away.*** Discuss the situation with your preferred advisor, or make an appointment to meet with the head of academic advising, the dean of your department, or another official that can help.

Your Responsibilities as an Advisee

It feels great to know you have options, and to exercise them. But you also have important responsibilities in the academic advising process. Your academic advisor is a knowledgeable, trained and experienced professional – but he/she isn't a mind reader. Being a responsible and conscientious advisee will help you get the most out of your academic advising experience. When you work with your academic advisor you should:

- ***Respect your academic advisor's schedule and time.*** If you cannot meet during the times your advisor has designated, discuss the situation with your advisor and see if other times can work for both of you.
- ***Schedule your meetings with your advisor well in advance*** to give yourself plenty of time to prepare before you make important decisions about class registration, choice of major, etc.
- ***Come prepared to your meetings*** with your advisor. Ask your advisor what you should bring. Bring a list of questions you would like to ask, as well as your calendar or planner and a copy of your latest transcripts.
- ***Arrive early.***
- ***Ask a lot of questions.***
- ***Take notes.***
- ***Ask for clarification*** if you are unclear about anything discussed during the meeting.

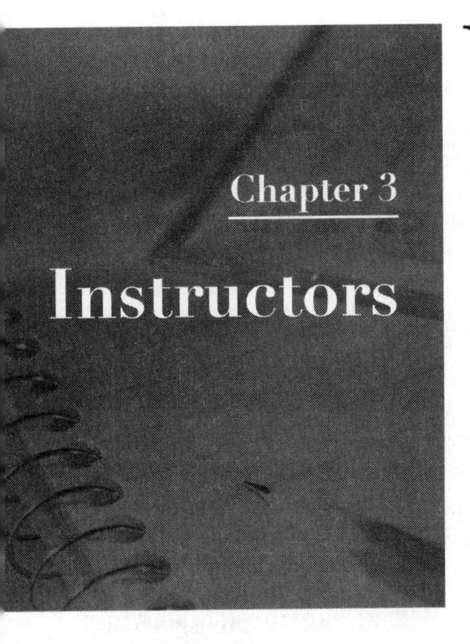

Chapter 3

Instructors

You have relationships with your parents, siblings and friends that you have developed through communication, understanding and mutual respect. Now, as a new college student, you will also need to develop relationships with your instructors. And, much like your other relationships, these student/teacher relationships will be built on communication, understanding and respect.

Many students are intimidated by instructors and are afraid that their instructors will judge them, they will appear to other students to be a "teacher's pet," or become a bother to their instructors if they try to develop a relationship. This couldn't be farther from the truth. In fact, if you fail to develop relationships with your instructors you will miss out on opportunities to greatly aid your learning process and deepen your college experience. An instructor with whom you have a great relationship can serve as a mentor and offer you:

- ***Advice on how to do better in class*** – and in college in general.
- ***Their trust*** and, therefore, the benefit of the doubt when your answer on an exam or assignment is in question.
- ***Inside information and recommendations for employment opportunities*** – both during and after college.
- ***Valuable contacts in the industry*** or area of interest in which you wish to pursue a career.
- ***Help in determining career goals.***
- ***An invitation to be a teaching or research assistant.***
- ***Recommendation letters and references*** for graduate school admission or a post-graduation job.

While most instructors are very intelligent and busy people, they are working as instructors because they want to teach students and serve as a mentor while you learn. They expect their students to get to know them and use them as learning resources. It is, however, up to you to initiate your student/instructor relationship and take advantage of the resources your instructors can offer.

This chapter will help you develop positive and valuable relationships with your instructors by:

- Helping you understand the kinds of instructors you may have.
- Explaining ways you can develop effective relationships with instructors.
- Recommending strategies for dealing with difficult instructors.

Different Kinds of Instructors

All instructors are not the same. In fact, at most colleges there are a variety of types of instructors, all with varying levels of education and teaching experience. Here's a brief run-down of the kinds of instructors you are likely to encounter during your college years:

Professors – Professors are the instructor all-stars. They are the highest-ranking instructors because they have earned a doctoral degree and have fulfilled the requirements for tenure. Tenure means different things at different colleges, but usually it means that candidates have completed a regime of teaching, research, writing and college/community service on which they are evaluated and granted tenure for their success by a college committee.

Associate/Assistant Professors – These instructors are in the process of earning their doctoral degrees and tenure status. Some may have just begun the process, while others may be close to becoming full-fledged professors.

Adjunct Instructors – Also called lecturers, adjunct instructors are not full-time instructors and are not in consideration for tenure. They are hired by the college to teach various courses and usually have extensive experience in the subjects they teach. Some adjunct instructors may even be professionals in the field in which they teach. For example, an adjunct instructor of an introductory accounting course may actually work as an accountant in addition to his/her teaching duties. Adjuncts may or may not have an advanced degree, and may or may not be considering a career as a professor.

Teaching Assistants – Also referred to as graduate teaching assistants or assistant instructors, they are typically students pursuing advanced degrees in the subject they teach. For example, if the instructor of your chemistry lab is a teaching assistant, he or she is most likely working toward earning a master's or doctorate degree in chemistry or another related science subject. In many cases, these students are required to teach as part of their degree requirements and may receive in, exchange for their teaching work, a small stipend or a waiver of tuition fees or expenses.

Developing a Relationship in Class

Your instructor/student relationships start in the classroom. During class, instructors are able to identify the students who seem interested, enthusiastic, and committed to success. To make sure you are one of these students:

- ***Attend class and arrive on time.*** If you must miss class, let your instructor know when and why you missed class and ask how you can make up the information learned during that class.
- ***Participate.*** Class discussions are a great way to express your opinions and ideas, and to ask questions and clarify points. A great way to stand out during class discussions is to identify how course materials relate to current events or the real world.
- ***Ask questions.*** Your instructors gauge how well students are learning and which areas need to be given more emphasis by paying attention to what kinds of questions are being asked. Some students might think that asking questions might make them seem stupid, but asking questions actually has the opposite effect. A well-crafted question can actually demonstrate a student's good grasp of the subject and show a deeper thought process that is impressive to instructors. Also, avoid questions like, "Will this be on the exam?" These kinds of questions make students look like they are more interested in the exam than in the subject.
- ***Prepare well for class*** by completing all assignments and reading. This includes turning in all assignments on time and showing up for all quizzes and exams.
- ***Don't be disruptive or attract negative attention*** from your instructor by talking with other students, talking on a cell phone, eating or drinking, or leaving class early.
- ***Sit in the front of the class.***

- ***Address your instructor correctly and with respect.*** At the beginning of the term, your instructor will let you know how they would like to be addressed and how to pronounce their name correctly. Make sure you do!
- ***Show respect for other students' – and your instructor's – opinions and views.*** Don't interrupt during discussions or say anything demeaning or disrespectful.

Developing a Relationship Outside of Class

Class is a great place to develop a relationship with your instructor, but you also have other opportunities to get to know your instructors outside of class. Take advantage of these opportunities. Here's how:

- ***Take advantage of office hours.*** Most instructors maintain office hours or periods of time when they are available, in their office, to meet with students – with our without appointments.
- ***Make an appointment.*** Even if you are not required to, you should try to make an appointment to meet with your instructor during office hours. Making an appointment demonstrates to your instructor that the meeting is important to you and that you value their time.
- ***Start early.*** Schedule meetings with your instructors as early in the day as possible, before your instructor becomes tired or distracted by the day's work. The early rule also applies to early in the term – by the end of the term instructors are overrun with students wishing to talk about their grades. The earlier in the term you begin meeting with your instructor, the better off you will be.
- ***Be punctual and prepared.*** Always be on time to appointments with your instructor and arrive prepared with an agenda of information you would like to cover, topics you would like to discuss and questions you need to ask. Bring all relevant assignments, notes, books and materials. If you must be late, call and let your instructor know.
- ***Avoid meeting with instructors right after class.*** There will be other students vying for their attention and you won't be able to get the attention you need.
- ***Get involved.*** Many instructors also lead clubs or serve as mentors for clubs or student groups. Participating in these activities is a great way to develop relationships with instructors who you already have or might have in the future. For example, if you think you will choose English as your major, join the staff of the college literary magazine. Chances are some of the best and most committed English instructors serve as advisors for this publication.

- ***Pay attention to extracurricular events.*** Instructors don't spend all of their time teaching. In fact, much of a college instructor's time is spent writing, researching and pursuing other activities related to their field. If you make a habit of checking campus and community events and activities, you will probably find that many of your current, past and future professors regularly appear in public to give readings of books they have published, participate in talks, debates or panel discussions, present research findings, offer special tours of area museums or points of interest that fall under their subject area, and lead special classes, lectures and activities that relate to their role as an expert in their field. Even if one of your instructors is not leading one of these programs, they may attend and participate. Participating in activities like these can help you meet and get to know instructors in your major, as well as broaden your learning experience.

Dealing with Difficult Instructors

Unfortunately, it is highly unlikely that you will love every instructor that you have during your college career. Some you will find boring, others may be hard to learn from, and still others may be intimidating, eccentric or opinionated. There are as many kinds of people working as instructors as there are fish in the sea, and you won't like every one. Believe it or not, every one of your instructors may not be crazy about you either!

That doesn't mean, however, that you will fail to succeed when you don't "click" with your instructor. In fact, part of what you will learn in college is how to work with different kinds of people – even ones you don't like – and still succeed. It will be a skill that will serve you well in the real world.

When you find one of your instructors difficult to work with:

Do:

- ***Contact other students.*** Find other students who have taken courses taught by the instructor in question and ask for advice on how best to work with this instructor – and what pitfalls to avoid.
- ***Show interest.*** Instructors appreciate when students are interested and enthusiastic about their course. Showing interest will make your instructor more likely to offer help.
- ***Support your hard work with evidence.*** When meeting with an instructor that you find difficult, come prepared and bring evidence that shows you are committed to the class. Such evidence can include completed assignments or notes.
- ***Use instructor evaluation sheets effectively.*** Many colleges require instructors to distribute evaluation sheets to all students at the end of

the term. These evaluations are usually anonymous (*meaning you don't have to put your name on them*), and are used to help instructors identify their strengths and weaknesses and get better at their job. Sometimes these evaluations are even used during departmental reviews of the instructors' performance. Don't use evaluations as a way to vent negative feelings or punish instructors. Instead, honestly evaluate instructors and try to give feedback that can help them change for the better.

Don't:

- ***Take it personally.*** Instructors are only human. Sometimes they have a bad day, or are going through a tough time in their life. Some instructors are poor communicators, have unusual teaching styles, or just don't "click" with certain students. If you feel that your instructor is difficult, don't take it personally. It is highly unlikely that the instructor is targeting you or singling you out for bad treatment. Chances are other students find this instructor's style difficult as well. Keeping this in mind will help you deal with the instructor fairly and keep things in perspective.
- ***Be negative.*** You will accomplish nothing by adopting a negative attitude, reacting harshly or giving up. Instead of dwelling on what you don't like about an instructor or class, focus on what you can do to improve the situation and make the experience a good one.
- ***Be vague or general.*** When speaking with or meeting with your instructor, make sure you have specific questions, and stay on topic. Telling your instructor you "just don't understand" doesn't help him/her to understand where you are having problems, and can make a bad situation worse. Instead, identify specific areas and questions you would like to address and stick to them.
- ***Ignore the problem.*** If you truly believe that the relationship between you and your instructor is affecting your grade, make an appointment to meet with your academic advisor for advice.

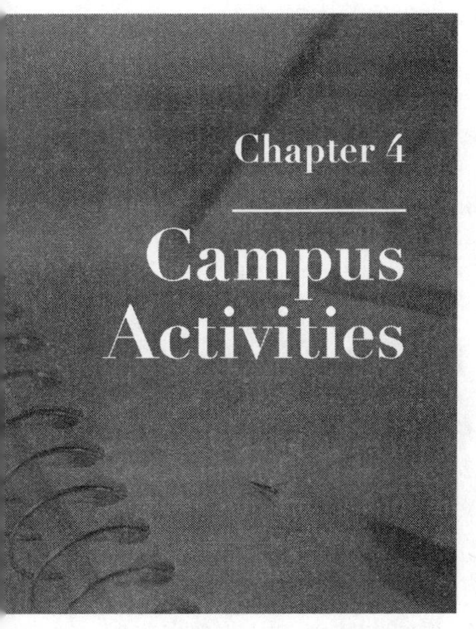

When most students think about college, they think about classes, instructors, exams, studying and grades. They probably don't think about playing basketball, running for public office, rock climbing, organizing a food drive, or planning a homecoming party. But all of these activities are a vital part of college too. Why? Because there is a whole world of campus activities waiting for you – from student government, to groups such as the debate club, to a variety of service organizations. In fact, in colleges all across the country, campus activities are as plentiful and diverse as the interests of students themselves.

So, should you join a campus activity? Why? And how do you choose what to take part in?

This chapter will answer these questions and help you understand the world of campus activities by:

- Explaining the reasons why being active in campus activities can be a great experience.
- Describing common types of campus activities.
- Recommending strategies for choosing an activity that's right for you.

Why Get Involved?

Aside from the fun you will have, there are a lot of great reasons to get involved in campus activities. Campus activities are a great way to:

- ***Grow your circle of friends and valuable contacts.***
- ***Get to know college faculty and staff.***
- ***Develop strengths*** that are important to your future, like skills in leadership, management, communication and networking.
- ***Build your resume.*** Showing that you were active and committed to a variety of activities outside of your coursework is a great way to impress potential employers.
- ***Learn.*** Your entire college experience is a learning experience – including the activities you choose!

Of course, just like everything else, when it comes to campus activities, you get out of them what you put in. Before joining any campus activity, make sure it will be a positive, enriching experience by committing to:

- ***Attending meetings*** and events regularly.
- ***Showing up on time*** for meetings and activities.
- ***Being active*** during meetings and projects.
- ***Providing leadership*** by volunteering for larger roles in the organization.

Types of Campus Activities

As mentioned before, there are as many on-campus activities as there are student interests. Most activities can be classified by one of the following descriptions:

Sports – From intercollegiate sports to intramural sports to specially formed on-campus teams, leagues and tournaments, most colleges have a wide variety of sports teams and activities available. Sports can include everything from football, basketball and lacrosse to skiing, skydiving and bowling.

Student Government – Nearly every college has a student government. These organizations can include elected offices like president, vice-president and treasurer, as well as appointed roles such as cabinet director or ambassador.

Journalism – Most colleges have a student-published newspaper. Many even have student-run radio stations, television networks and magazines.

Academic Clubs and Societies – Some of these clubs have stringent membership requirements, such as honor societies. Others only require you to be interested in the subject – for example, an astronomy club, French club, or literary group.

Political – It's no secret that colleges have long been a hotbed of political activism. So it's no surprise that political groups and clubs abound on college campuses. From Amnesty International and Greenpeace to College Republicans and College Democrats, chances are your college will have an activity for you, no matter which way your politics lean.

Culture and Identity – Some campus groups are formed based on the culture or identity of its members. Latino student associations and international student organizations are a couple examples.

Special-Interest Groups – These groups are based on the common interests of its members. Photography clubs, science clubs, mountain biking groups and performing arts organizations are just a few examples of special-interest groups.

Greek System – Fraternities and sororities make up the Greek system. These organizations vary in their role, size, mission and traditions from college to college, but mainly act as a social outlet to counterbalance the rigors of school.

Religious – Many different religious affiliations are represented in on-campus groups, including Christianity, Judaism, Islam and Buddhist.

Choose an Activity That's Right for You

As a new college student, you are probably excited and enthusiastic about the opportunities available to you. You may be interested in photography and French culture, have aspirations to represent your class as a student senator, and be inspired to explore your political and spiritual beliefs. But, before you join the photography club and French club, put your name on the ballot and sign up for Amnesty International and the Christian Student Association, there are a few things you need to ask yourself:

What Is Your Motivation And Goal?
Explore your reasons for wanting to take part in an activity. Do you want to make more friends, develop a new skill, or just relax and enjoy yourself? Defining your motivations and goals can help you narrow your choices. For example, if the math club regularly competes at high-stress tournaments and you are simply looking for a club where you can make friends and have fun, this activity may not be for you.

Does The Activity Fit Your Needs?
Once you know why you want to join an activity, you can begin your search for the activity that meets your needs. Do your homework on the club, group or activity to make sure you fully understand the mission, values and requirements of the organization. To find out more about on-campus activities at your college:

- ***Ask other students*** about activities and organizations that may interest you.
- ***Meet with your academic advisor*** and ask for recommendations.
- ***Visit your student activities center*** and ask for a list of activities. Your college Web site and catalog may include lists of available activities as well.
- ***Attend a campus activity fair.*** Many colleges hold regular events where representatives from student organizations can teach interested students more about their organization and encourage them to join.
- ***Go to a meeting.*** Throughout the year many student organizations will host "new member" meetings. Keep an eye on bulletin boards and campus publications to find these meetings.

Can You Fulfill the Requirements?

Different campus organizations have different requirements. Make sure you are able to fulfill the academic, financial, time and other requirements before you decide to join. A few requirements to consider:

- ***Initiation fees, dues and other costs.*** While they are usually well worth it, membership in clubs, organizations and activities sometimes comes with a financial burden. Some clubs levy a hefty initiation fee, while others charge yearly dues. And don't forget about the uniforms you may have to buy for sports teams, the money you may have to spend to travel to club activities, tournaments or regional meetings, materials and equipment you may have to purchase, and other funds you may need to pay to be a fully active member.
- ***Minimum participation requirements.*** Organizations don't want members who don't participate or fail to show up for meetings and activities. To encourage involvement, organizations may take attendance and require that members attend a minimum number of meetings or put in a minimum number of hours of activity with the club.
- ***Minimum grade point averages.*** Many colleges mandate that students must maintain a minimum grade point average in order to be members of extracurricular clubs. Even if your college does not require it, organizations may insist that members maintain good grades for continued membership.
- ***Completion of a specific task.*** Some groups require members to complete a specific series of tasks, pass a test or demonstrate a certain skill level. A scuba diving club, for example, may require its members to be licensed scuba divers, or become licensed within a certain amount of time. Service organizations may require you to volunteer a specific number

of hours in order to be initiated. French clubs may require potential members to pass an oral test in the language.

- ***Equipment.*** Many sports activities require you to own your own equipment, such as a stick for lacrosse, a glove for baseball, even a horse for the equestrian club! Other non-sports clubs may require you to have materials as well, such as a computer for the computer club or a camera for the photography club.

One last note on campus activities: don't forget why you are in college. While joining organizations and getting involved in activities is a great way to get the most out of your college experience, if your education suffers because of it you may need to rethink your choices. Choose wisely. Make sure the activities and organizations you do join offer you many benefits without taking away from your academic achievement.

First, the good news. Colleges across America spend millions of dollars and tons of effort each year to ensure that students are safe and campus environments are tough on crime. Highly trained campus police forces, state-of-the-art security systems, cutting-edge crime curbing techniques and expensive lighting, walkways and nighttime student escort services are just a few of the measures that many colleges take to make sure you are as safe as possible.

The bad news is that hundreds of thousands of college students will become victims of crimes this year. Theft, carjacking, stalking, sexual assault, even murder (*while fairly rare*), are not unheard of on college campuses. Your college is doing its part to make sure you don't become a crime victim. Now, you have to do your part.

This chapter will show you how by:

- Outlining basic, overall safety strategies every college student should implement.
- Describing specific strategies you can implement to ensure you won't become a victim of different kinds of crime.

Know the Basics

Research The Facts – Know current crime trends and problems on your campus and in the surrounding community. Watch the news, read the paper and pay attention to published crime reports. Colleges are required by law to report on-campus crimes to the federal government. You can research your college's crime statistics at the U.S. government's Web site: www.ope.ed.gov./security/search.asp.

Familiarize Yourself – Take the time to become familiar with your campus – know where well-lighted paths, emergency phones and campus police stations are located.

Share Your Schedule – Let roommates, friends and family know where you will be at all times so they can locate you when they need to.

Get to Know Law Enforcement – Find out what kinds of services your campus police offers, how you can contact them, and what their rules are regarding letting students carry self-defense items like pepper spray on campus.

Carry a Cell Phone – Experts say that one of the biggest deterrents to criminals is seeing that their potential victim has a cell phone. Carry one at all times, and think about carrying a whistle as well to alert people around you if you see or are the victim of a crime.

Take a Self-Defense Course – Your college or campus police force may offer these kinds of classes on an ongoing basis at little or no cost.

Be Aware – Most crimes happen when you are not paying attention. Be aware of your surroundings and look as if you have a purpose and know where you are heading. Pay attention to where your backpack, purse and other belongings are at all times.

Report Suspicious Activity – It's always better to be safe than sorry. Report anything you find suspicious to campus police – it could save someone, including yourself, from being a victim of a crime.

Don't Use ATMs After Dark – Get your cash while it's still light outside, and avoid using isolated ATMs. If you must visit an ATM after dark, make sure it is well lit, and don't go alone.

Don't Carry a Lot of Cash or Valuables – Don't make yourself a target by carrying or keeping large amounts of cash, expensive jewelry or big-ticket items like laptops and other valuables on your person or in your room if it isn't necessary. If you will be leaving your dorm room or apartment for an extended period of time, such as over spring break, remove your valuables and take them to a safe place.

Protect Your Privacy – Think twice about listing your picture, name and contact information in public areas such as your campus Web site or directory.

Give it Up – If you are confronted by a criminal who wants your valuables, give them up! No possession is worth risking your life for.

Protect Yourself

From Drug- And Alcohol-Related Crimes

Face the facts: drugs and alcohol are the chief factors in many personal health and safety problems during college. Drunk driving accidents, date rape, fights and overdoses are just a few devastating consequences of college students misusing and abusing drugs and alcohol. If you're still not convinced, consider these shocking – but true – statistics regarding college students between the ages of 18 and 24:

- Every year half a million people are unintentionally injured while under the influence of alcohol.
- More than 600,000 people are assaulted each year by another student who has been drinking.
- More than 70,000 people are victims of alcohol-related sexual assault or date rape.
- 400,000 people had unprotected sex and more than 100,000 report being too intoxicated to know if they consented to having sex.
- 2.1 million people drove under the influence of alcohol.
- 110,000 people are arrested for an alcohol-related violation, like public drunkenness or driving under the influence.
- 1,400 people die from alcohol-related unintentional injuries, including car crashes.

Using drugs and alcohol leaves college students vulnerable to a variety of crimes, accidents and negative circumstances that are usually avoidable. Don't let it happen to you! If you find yourself in a situation where alcohol or drugs are being used, leave. If you believe others may be at risk, contact the proper authorities. You could save someone's life.

From Sexual Assault And Rape

Sexual assault and rape are devastating, but seldom talked about, hazards of college life. A large number of sexual assaults and rapes are reported on college campuses each year – but experts believe that the crimes that are reported are only a small percentage of the total number of sexual assaults and rapes actually committed. Unfortunately, many victims are too embarrassed or scared to report their experiences.

Don't become a statistic. You can reduce your risk of sexual assault or rape by:

Knowing the facts:

- Alcohol and drugs are involved in nearly half of all sexual assaults and rapes.
- More than sixty percent of sexual assault and rape victims know their attacker.
- Every forty-five seconds a woman in the United States is raped.
- Fewer than thirty percent of sex crimes are reported to the police.
- Nine out of ten rape victims are female.
- Most rapes are planned.
- Even if the victim knows the attacker, rape is still a crime.

Taking important measures:

- ***Go to parties in a group*** and vow to stay together and leave together.
- ***Keep your judgment clear*** – avoid alcohol and drugs.
- ***Don't ever leave a party with someone you don't know well*** – especially if you are under the influence of alcohol or drugs. Most victims of sexual assault and rape know their attacker.
- ***Get your own drink and keep it in your possession at all times*** to avoid having it laced with date rape drugs.
- ***Meet dates in a public place*** like a movie theater or restaurant.
- ***Date in groups or pairs*** until you get to know people well.
- ***Learn as much about your date as you can before you go out.***
- ***Carry a cell phone with you at all times*** – and keep it with you, not in your purse. If you feel you are in danger, call 911.
- ***Always carry plenty of cash*** on dates and to parties so you can pay your own way, or pay for a cab home if necessary.
- ***Avoid secluded places*** and be aware of your surroundings at all times.
- ***Trust your gut.*** If your instincts tell you that something isn't right, pay attention. Better safe than sorry.
- ***Assert yourself.*** Express yourself clearly and don't be afraid to say no.

From Theft

Theft is one of the most common crimes on college campuses. While instances of theft do not usually result in injury, it can be stressful, financially draining and personally devastating to lose money, valuable goods or treasured belongings. To reduce your chances of becoming a victim of theft:

- ***Keep your windows and doors locked at all times.***
- ***Memorize emergency telephone numbers*** or keep them easily accessible.
- ***Don't lend out your keys, access cards or entrance codes.***
- ***Don't announce your name on your voicemail.***
- ***Female students should ask a male to record their voicemail.***
- ***Don't indicate that you will be gone for a period of time*** on your door or on your voicemail.
- ***Get to know your neighbors*** and plan a system in which you can look out for each other.
- ***Leave a light or a radio on*** while you are away from your dorm or apartment – or invest in timers that turn lights or other electrical appliances on and off.
- ***Hide valuables*** – never leave them where they are visible.
- ***Try to vary your daily routine*** so thieves will have a difficult time predicting when you will be home and when you will not.
- ***Don't go alone to isolated places*** like laundry rooms, elevators or stairwells.

While Outside

To commit a crime, criminals need an opportunity. The more you can do to reduce these opportunities in your everyday life, the more you can reduce your risk of being a victim. Think about the time you spend outside and try to implement the following strategies to reduce your risk while walking, exercising and spending time outdoors:

- ***Travel in a group or in pairs.***
- ***Use well-lit and well-traveled walkways.***
- ***Know where emergency phones are located.***
- ***Use escort services and public transportation,*** if available. Even if it takes longer, it's safer.
- ***Walk quickly and with a purpose.*** Your body language can communicate to a would-be criminal that you are confident, able and know where you are going.
- ***Make wide turns in stairwells, hallways and between buildings*** so you can see people who are approaching you and following you.
- ***Avoid walking and exercising outside at night.*** If you must do these activities after dark, do them with a friend and choose routes ahead of time that are safe and well-populated.

- ***Register your bike with campus and/or community police,*** and always use a good bike lock.
- ***Don't wear headphones*** when you walk or bike. They limit your awareness.

While In Your Car

If you are a college student who is lucky enough to have a car with you at school, don't be unlucky enough to be a victim of an auto crime, like theft or carjacking. Many victims of muggings, kidnappings and sexual assaults are accosted while getting into their car. Use the following tips to reduce your risk:

- ***Make sure your parking spots are well-lit*** and close to your destination.
- ***Lock your doors and close your windows*** – both when you are driving and when the car is parked.
- ***Have your keys ready as you return to your car*** so you can enter the car immediately.
- ***Check the interior of your car before getting in*** to make sure nobody is inside.
- ***Keep valuables in the trunk*** where they are not readily visible. Better yet, don't keep valuables in your car at all.
- ***Make sure your vehicle is in good driving condition*** before you begin to drive.
- ***If someone threatens your safety in an attempt to steal your car, don't resist.*** Get out of the car and run to a safe place.

While Taking Public Transportation

Many college students use public transportation to travel to classes, meetings and social events. From small campus shuttles, to the large-scale bus and subway systems in large cities, public transportation is a great way to get where you need to go. But get there safely. Try the following strategies to keep yourself and your valuables free from harm:

- ***Don't wait at isolated bus or subway stops,*** especially at night.
- ***Sit near the driver on an empty bus.***
- ***Don't sit in empty train or subway cars.*** If a person on your car seems suspicious, move.
- ***Take a moment to find where emergency devices,*** like alarms and exits, are located on buses, trains and subways.
- ***Sit close to the exit.***

- ***Avoid fumbling with change or fare cards*** while entering public transportation – have your fare ready.
- ***Stay alert*** – don't nap or daydream while riding public transportation.
- ***Be wary of noisy passengers or other commotion.*** Sometimes criminals will use a distraction like this to help them steal your valuables.
- ***Make sure any cab you take is licensed and well-marked*** with a company name and contact information. Make note of the cab number and driver's name.
- ***Never share a cab with a stranger.***
- ***Insist that cabs drop you off in well-lit, populated areas.***
- ***If at any time you feel a cab is taking you anywhere other than your requested destination, speak up.*** If your concerns are not addressed, use your cell phone to call 911.

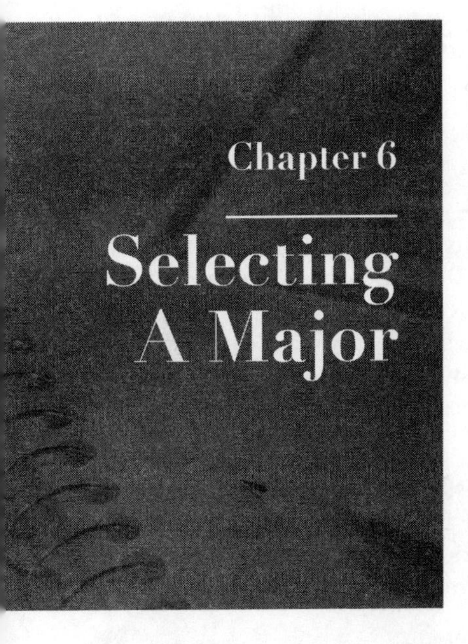

Some students enter college with a clear vision of what the focus of their study and future career will be. Other students start the first day of college classes without a clue about which course of study and kind of career path they will pursue. And other college students begin their college career with a solid idea of which major they will select, only to change their mind once, twice, even a few times over the course of their college years!

Whichever description fits you – don't worry. Selecting a major is a major decision (*no pun intended*). However, college isn't all about your major. Your college years are a time to experience new things, learn more about yourself and the world, discover what interests and inspires you, and make decisions about your future. However, the time will come when you will have to select and commit to a major.

This chapter will help you make this "major" decision easier by:

- Explaining the timeline for selecting a major.
- Recommending strategies for selecting a major that fits you.
- Outlining options in selecting a major, including changing your mind and selecting more than one focus.

When to Select a Major

The timeline for selecting a major differs with every college. Generally, you will be required to commit to a major by the end of your sophomore (*second*) year or the beginning of your junior (*third*) year. To learn about the specific requirements of your college, refer to your student handbook and meet with your academic advisor.

It's important not to rush the process of selecting a major. That said, you also should not wait until the last minute to make your decision. The earlier you decide on a major, the earlier you can begin taking the classes that are prerequisites for your major. Waiting too long to select might result in your taking unnecessary classes or too many electives, and can even extend the time it will take for you to graduate because you will begin taking necessary classes late in your college career.

Make the Right Decision

Some students spend many sleepless nights thinking about what major to select, only to make the wrong decision. Don't be one of these students. Selecting the right major is a delicate balance between selecting the subject area (*and resulting career*) that interests you, best uses your talents and skills, and helps you to fulfill your long-term lifestyle goals. While there is no one right way to go about selecting a major, there are a few things you can do to make it easier. Try these tips:

List The Subjects And Careers That Interest You
Start your decision process by making a detailed list of your interests. Start making this list early on in the process and edit it as your interests change or develop – it's okay to add or delete interests.

Evaluate The Requirements For Potential Majors
While some majors may interest you, you may change your mind when you learn the requirements. For example, you may think that a medical career interests you because you like helping people and enjoy science. But learning the stringent science – based requirements may deter you from selecting a pre-med course of study if you don't enjoy science. Refer to your college's course catalog or meet with your academic advisor to find out major requirements.

Take Courses That Interest You Early On
One way to try out areas of study that interest you is to take courses in these areas. Some colleges even allow students to "audit" classes, or take classes without earning credit. Take as many classes as you can in the areas that interest you – it's the best way to find out if the subject truly interests you. Talk with other students or meet with your advisor to find out which classes will give you a good overview of a subject.

Talk
What better way to find out more about a career that interests you than to talk to people who are currently working in the field? These contacts can

give you a complete picture of what their career is really like, offer you advice on how to get where you want to be, and give you insights on the downsides of their field. Find people in fields that interest you by contacting your college's career center or alumni association, by searching the Internet or phone book for local businesses in the field (*which is also a great way to learn about possible internships*), or speak with your instructors to find out if they have any contacts in the business world.

Get Involved
The best way to find out if something interests you is to get hands-on experience. Think you want to be a nurse? Volunteer in a hospital. Want to be a public relations executive? Secure an internship at a local agency. Find teaching intriguing? Try working part-time at a day care center. Visit your school's career center to find out more about volunteer, internship and employment opportunities that could help you find out more about your interests.

Test Your Aptitude
If you need more insight into your personality, talents and skills, taking an aptitude test might help you discover more about yourself, including which career areas would best suit you. College career centers often offer popular aptitude tests, or can refer you to a reputable testing center.

Consider The Career
Selecting a major that interests you is great. However, you also have to consider the career paths that your chosen major will lead you down. The content of business management classes may fascinate you, but if the thought of leading, advising and managing people terrifies you, a career in business management may not be for you. Before selecting a major, carefully consider how you would fit into the resulting careers.

- ***Evaluate your personality.*** How does your personality suit the career path that results from your major? Are you a people person, or do you prefer working with numbers and facts? Are you a team player or someone who works better alone? Are you someone who thrives on change or craves routine?
- ***Assess education requirements.*** You can begin many careers once you receive your college diploma. However, others require more education – two, four, six, even seven or more years of classes, residencies, apprenticeships and so on! Of course, additional education can be a plus in any career, but for some, such as medical sciences and law, it is a requirement. Look into education requirements and think about whether you are up to more schooling before you leap.
- ***Think about location.*** Consider where you would like to live. For example, if you envision yourself living in Montana, then a career in

marine biology is not for you. Want to work in publishing? Most likely you'll have to live in New York City or another thriving metropolis.

- ***To travel or not to travel.*** Travel sounds like a career perk, but it can also be a difficult lifestyle. If your dream is to settle down, have a family and coach your son's baseball team, then a career that requires extensive travel – such as a pilot – might not be the best choice for you.
- ***Consider career conditions.*** Doctors are on call all hours of the night. Accountants work long hours during tax season. Preschool teachers are exposed to all kinds of childhood illnesses. Advertising copywriters are required to be creative and work on tight deadlines. Police officers are required to enforce laws and follow procedures. None of these on-the-job conditions may bother you. On the other hand, all of them might. Research and understand the real conditions and environments of the career you are considering before making a commitment to a major.
- ***Evaluate earning power.*** Money is important to everyone, of course, but just how important is money to you? Some career paths have very high earning potentials, while others practically guarantee that you will never be rich. You can find out the potential earning power of the careers that interest you online at a variety of career Web sites. Think very carefully about the kind of lifestyle you would like to have and what kind of sacrifices you are willing to make before you commit to a career path with a lower earning power. On the other hand, remember that money isn't everything, and a high salary will be little comfort if you are miserable when you go to work every day.
- ***Think about leadership ability.*** Are you a born leader, or do you shy away from taking charge? Many careers demand that you posses strong leadership skills – business management and teaching come to mind. If you are not a leader, there are still plenty of career choices that require less leadership ability or none at all.

If You Can't Decide

You may find that you cannot decide between one or more areas in which you have a strong interest. Or, to your dismay, you may find that you have selected a major, but have selected poorly. Don't wallow in your unhappiness – do something! You have a few options:

Change Your Major

As mentioned before, changing majors is not unheard of. Many students select a major, but later take a class, participate in an activity, complete an internship or take a part-time job that exposes them to new areas of interest and makes them decide to pursue a new major. Sometimes this change is a minor one – from earth science to biology, for example. Other students may change their major dramatically – from business to teaching, or physics to communications. While changing majors can delay your graduation date, it is always an option. Meeting with your academic advisor is the first step toward changing your major. Your advisor will help you with the process of changing your major, advise you on the requirements of your new major, and let you know what kind of delay or consequences – if any – this change will cause. Just keep in mind that indecisiveness or rash decisions can lead to unnecessary and additional tuition, time and effort.

Select A Double Major Or A Minor

Some students who can't select a major don't. They select two! It's true: most colleges offer students the opportunity to pursue two major courses of study. Double majors can maximize your education and improve your employment prospects. On the other hand, double majors can be difficult, demanding and time consuming. Another option is to select a minor, which does not have quite as many requirements. Before committing to a double major or minor, consider the following:

- ***Decide early.*** If a double major or minor is for you, try to make the decision as early as possible in order to minimize the time it will take you to complete your requirements and graduate. The earlier you can develop a course schedule streamlined for your areas of study, the better off you will be.
- ***Limit your electives.*** Because of the number of classes that are required to fulfill a double major or major/minor, the number of electives you will be able to take will be reduced.
- ***Select well.*** When selecting your two majors or your major and minor, make sure the two work together and create realistic and interesting career choices. For example, a double major of communications and graphic design would make you a very appealing job candidate – an employee who can write, communicate and create visual concepts for advertising or public relations campaigns. A double major of the two unrelated subjects of biology and theater may be less appealing – in fact, it can even appear as a sign of indecisiveness to potential employers.

The first time you take a look at your college's course catalog, you may be overwhelmed. Which classes do you have to take? Which ones do you want to take? Which instructors are the best? Will the classes you need and want be available? How will you fit them all into your day – and into four years?

Choosing and registering for your classes may seem like a formality, but these are actually some of the most important choices you will make during your college years. Deciding which classes to take, which instructors to take them from, when to take them, and how you will fit them together like puzzle pieces is no easy task, and your decisions are important. The choices you make about your schedule will shape what you learn, how you learn it, how long it will take you to graduate, and quite possibly the course your future will take. Make the right decisions!

This chapter will show you how by:

- Showing you how to develop a plan.
- Recommending strategies for choosing classes and instructors.
- Giving you tips on how to develop a schedule that works.
- Letting you know how to deal with the registration process.

Develop a Graduation Plan

Developing a schedule for one term without thinking about how it fits into the big picture is like trying to build a house without blueprints. You can build a great garage, but if it's on the second floor, how will you drive your car into it? You can take a full schedule of perfectly wonderful classes, but if they don't fulfill any requirements or help you to develop skills you will need in your major, then what's the point? Before you develop your schedule, you need to develop a graduation plan that works for you.

The first step in developing your graduation plan is to meet with your academic advisor. During your meeting you should discuss your goals, possible majors, classes that interest you, and your graduation timeline. Make sure you listen and ask lots of questions. Your advisor has years of experience and knowledge, and will be an invaluable resource as you navigate the scheduling jungle.

Using the advice your advisor has given you, you should develop a graduation plan that includes all of the classes you need and want to take and a timeline for when you should take these classes. If you haven't chosen a major yet, don't panic. Your timeline isn't written in stone, and should evolve and change as you progress.

As you develop your graduation plan, remember these tips:

Use The Course Catalog As A Guide
Your college course catalog may provide sample graduation schedules that you can use as a guide – a great building block for your graduation plan.

Pay Attention To Prerequisites
To take certain classes, you have to take others first. Don't make the mistake of getting to your junior year and realizing that you have forgotten to take some of the prerequisite classes for the classes you would like to – and need to – take.

Make Sure You Don't Miss Out
Many classes are not offered every term. Some classes are offered on a rotating basis – first level first term; second level second term. Others classes that are not in high demand may be offered only once a year. Still other classes are only offered sporadically, as qualified visiting professors become available. Your course catalog may make note of these classes. Take note so you don't miss out on a class you have your heart set on.

Avoid Overload – And Underachievement
Don't load yourself up with only difficult classes in one term. On the other hand, try to avoid taking too easy of a schedule. You should strive to develop a good mix of easy and difficult classes so that you are challenged, but not overwhelmed.

Introduce Yourself
As you are deciding on a major, take some introductory classes in subject areas you are considering. Your schedule should have room for you to take

a few electives without delaying your graduation date. Use these to explore and discover your interests.

Do The Math When It Comes To Credits
Don't take too many or too few credits in a term. Too many may spread you too thin and result in poor performance; too few may delay your graduation date.

Consider Summer School
To reduce class sizes during the school year, many colleges encourage students to take classes during the summer by offering great classes at convenient times. Take advantage of this option and you will give yourself more flexibility in your schedule during the school year, more chances to explore different subject areas, and possibly even the opportunity to make up for lost time or to graduate early.

Selecting Your Classes

You have a plan. Now you need to choose your classes. Here's how:

Know The Requirements
You will be required to complete a minimum number of classes is certain general subject areas such as math, English and science. These classes must meet minimum skill levels. In other words, you can't just take the easiest classes available to fulfill your requirements.

Find Your Level
You should start at a class level with which you are comfortable. Your academic advisor should be able to evaluate your academic history and recommend appropriate class levels in each subject area. You may even be required to take a placement exam to determine your knowledge level.

Consider Taking The "Challenge"
After meeting with an advisor and/or taking a placement exam, some students find that they have been placed in a lower-level class than expected. If this happens to you, you should think carefully about your best course of action. But keep in mind, for example, that completing a year of high-school French does not necessarily mean you will succeed in a higher-level college French class. However, if after evaluating your abilities, you still believe a mistake has been made, many colleges offer you the option to "challenge" a class. You will be required to take an exam developed by the instructor of the lower level class you would like to skip that covers the materials that would have been presented in the class. If you pass this exam, you may be given credit for the class and allowed to move on to the higher-level class. Keep in mind that a fee may be charged for this challenge process, and you may have to pay the fee even if you do not pass the exam.

Get The Facts
Carefully review your college course catalog for class descriptions. If you want more information, contact the department the class falls under or the instructor who teaches the class.

Consult With The Experts
Who are the biggest experts on which classes make the grade? Other students just like you! When you are considering classes, speak with students who have taken the classes to get their opinions. For a more objective opinion, you can also meet with your academic advisor.

Take Reviews With A Grain Of Salt
Some colleges provide publications that feature student reviews of classes, and many student Web sites and Web logs also include information and opinions about classes. Reviews like these can be helpful, but keep in mind that another student's viewpoint may not be your own. Try to get information about classes from a variety of sources before you make your decisions.

Have A Back-Up Plan
Remember the drop/add period that was discussed in the Selecting A Major chapter? This is a period of a few days at the beginning of the term during which you are permitted to drop classes from your schedule and add new ones. The drop/add period is a great time to test out classes you are unsure of without penalty by attending a class or two and seeing how you feel about the instructor, the content, the time, or location and so on. It may be a good idea to have a few extra classes in the back of your mind to add in case a class or an instructor doesn't turn out to be what you expected. Some students even register for an extra class to begin with, giving them the flexibility of dropping the class that appeals to them the least during the drop/add period.

Selecting Your Instructors

Believe it or not, the instructor you choose may be more important than the actual class. In the hands of a creative, passionate and experienced instructor, a class that you are not looking forward to may actually turn out to be enjoyable and enriching. Conversely, a class in your favorite subject can be a source of frustration if an instructor with whom you don't see eye-to-eye teaches it. Your choice of instructors is limited, and it will be impossible to love every single instructor you take. However, you can do a few things to ensure that you choose the instructors who are best for you:

Think About Your Learning Style
Do you like to learn by doing? Do vibrant class discussions deepen your understanding or intimidate you? Do you like working in groups or alone?

If you have a good understanding of how you learn best, it will be easier to choose instructors who fit your style. For example, if you learn best by talking about issues, then an instructor who lectures for the entire class and discourages student participation may not be for you.

Talk

One of the best ways to get the scoop on instructors is to talk with other students who have taken a class from the instructor. Get a few opinions and then make your own decision.

Know That Less Is Sometimes More

Introductory classes are often taught by associate instructors or teaching assistants. While these kinds of instructors are less experienced, this does not necessarily mean that their classes will be less valuable. In fact, associate instructors and teaching assistants are often more enthusiastic about the subject matter, less jaded by the teaching process, and able to offer you more time and help than instructors who have been teaching for years. If, however, you are concerned about the quality of instruction you will receive from a specific instructor, make an appointment to meet with them to get a sense of their teaching style, personality and knowledge.

Consider The Format, Not Just The Content

Do your research and find out how the classes you are considering are formatted. Are there two exams or four? Is class participation and attendance part of the grade? Are assignments done solo or in groups? What you will learn in the course is important, but how you will learn is an even bigger indicator of whether you will enjoy the class and succeed.

Choose To Be Challenged

Picking an instructor because you have heard he/she is an easy grader is not always the best option. The best college instructors challenge and inspire their students. You may find that the "easiest" instructors are also the most boring and the least likely to give you a valuable learning experience.

Developing Your Schedule

You've considered the classes. You've evaluated the instructors. Now you've got to make your choices fit into a neat little package that will be your schedule for the term. A few things to consider while creating your schedule:

Consider Commitments And Circumstances

Think about your work schedule, extracurricular activities, family commitments and anything else you may have going on during the term, then plan your schedule accordingly. For example, if you your sister is getting married and you are the maid of honor, you've promised your part-time job that you will pick up an extra shift every week, and your intramural soccer team is traveling to a week-long tournament – all during the upcoming term – then it's probably not the right time to take a full schedule of your most challenging classes.

Time Your Schedule Correctly
Are you a morning person? Take your classes in the morning when you are most alert. Can't think straight until noon? Afternoon and evening classes are for you.

Strive For Balance
Try to balance your weekly schedule so you are not maxed out on certain days. Too many classes scheduled for one day can make it more difficult to adequately prepare for class and maintain good study habits.

Take A Break
Try to schedule a break between classes during which you can review what you have just learned, prepare for your next class, grab something to eat, or just relax.

Don't Discount Distance
It may sound silly, but how far you have to travel from one class to another really does make a difference! If you only have ten minutes between classes and the classrooms are all the way across campus from each other, you may have to be a star sprinter to make it on time! Some classes are even held at satellite locations, making it necessary to drive or take public or campus transportation. Don't put yourself in this position – account for travel time in your schedule.

Avoid Registration Delays
Don't make the scheduling process even more difficult by procrastinating. Here are a few things to keep in mind to ensure you don't have any unneeded delays while developing your schedule:

- ***Visit, research and re-check*** – in plenty of time. Give yourself plenty of time to do the things you need to develop your schedule – meet with your advisor, research classes and instructors, and check for last-minute changes to the course catalog. The earlier you do these things, the better.
- ***Pay up.*** Many colleges will not allow students to register for the next term unless their balances for prior terms are paid in full. Sometimes something as small as a library fine of a few dollars can put a hold on your ability to register! Don't get to the final step of the scheduling process just to find out that an errant bill is standing in between you and the perfect schedule. Check your account balance ahead of time and pay up, if necessary.

- ***Be online savvy.*** Online class registration is available at many colleges these days and can be a convenient way to create your schedule. Just make sure you understand the online process so that you avoid any delays or mistakes.
- ***Get approval.*** Some colleges require students to get their schedules approved by their academic advisor before they can register. Other times you may be required to get an instructor's signature to indicate you have met the prerequisites or other standards to be accepted into a class. Get these approvals ahead of time – tracking down busy advisors and instructors just hours before registration ends is not fun!
- ***Be first in line.*** Most colleges allow students to register based on seniority – the most senior students are allowed to register first; the newest students going last. Find out when you are allowed to register, and then register at the earliest time possible. For example, if you are allowed to register from 8 a.m. to 5 p.m. on a given day, make sure you are registering at 8 a.m. – not at 4 p.m.

Remember that Filled Classes aren't Always Closed

Unfortunately, you may sometimes find that a class you want or need has filled up before you are able to register for it. When a class is filled up, the course is said to be "closed." If this happens to you, there are a few tricks you can pull out of your sleeve before switching to plan B:

- ***Plead your case with the instructor.*** Sometimes instructors impose their own class size limit, and may be willing to accommodate another student. Keep in mind that telling the instructor that their class fits perfectly into the schedule you have designed to allow yourself to sleep until noon is less effective than letting the instructor know how interested you are in the content of the class and how much you were looking forward to experiencing their teaching style.
- ***Attend and see.*** Other instructors may allow you to attend the class and see if you can be added as registered students drop the class during the drop/add period.
- ***Do the switch.*** You may even be able to register for another open section of the course, but attend the lecture of the closed class. Make sure to check with the instructor before you attempt this switch – you should confirm that the lectures and content covered for the two sections are identical. You will also need to find out whether you will be able to attend exam dates for the closed class you will be attending or for the section of the class for which you registered.

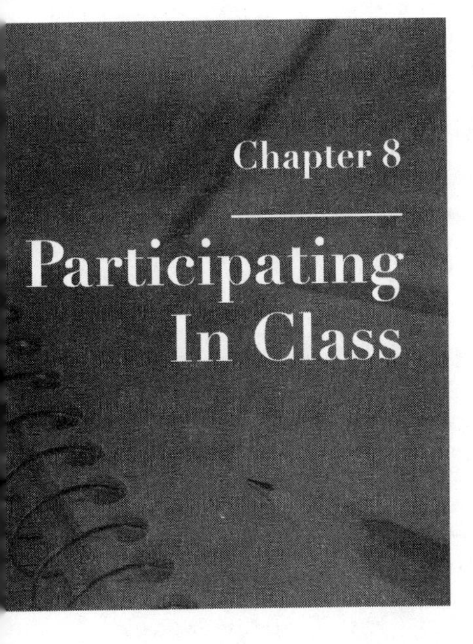

Chapter 8

Participating In Class

Participating in class can be intimidating for new college students. During the first year of college, many students avoid participating in class because they:

- ***Worry about what their classmates and instructor will think of them.***
- ***Are uncomfortable with public speaking.***
- ***Fear their classmates or instructor will think their questions or answers are dumb.***
- ***Assume that other students will consider them a "nerd" or a "brown-noser."***

These feelings are normal. In fact, your classmates are probably experiencing the same feelings you are. However, no matter what your reasons are for avoiding class participation, they are not justified. Class participation is an essential part of the college learning experience. Attending college without participating is like getting only half of what you paid for. Keep in mind that your hard work and dedication have earned you the right to be in college and that you are paying tuition to have access to your instructors. Make the most of your investment and time by becoming an active class participant.

This chapter will show you how by:

- Explaining the importance of class participation.
- Outlining the things you should and shouldn't do when participating in class.

Why Class Participation Matters

Class participation is extremely important for you, your classmates and your instructor because it:

- ***Demonstrates to your instructor that you are paying attention*** and completing assignments.
- ***Provides your instructors with valuable feedback*** on their teaching abilities.
- ***Helps instructors gauge the class' progress*** and understanding of the course materials.
- ***Helps you and other students with the learning process*** by stimulating discussion.
- ***Increases your concentration*** and helps you to stay focused on the information being presented.
- ***Is often an important component of your grade*** that can make the difference between earning a B or an A.
- ***Makes your class experience more enjoyable.***
- ***Increases your self-confidence.***
- ***Helps you develop public speaking skills.***
- ***Fosters a positive relationship*** between you and your instructor, and between you and your classmates.

Successful Class Participation

Participating in class can be difficult. Make it easier by practicing the following guidelines:

Do:

- ***Review class notes*** and complete assignments to prepare for each class.
- ***Anticipate questions*** your instructor may ask and develop answers ahead of time.
- ***Develop questions*** to ask for each class.
- ***Consider participating early in the class discussion*** – more difficult questions tend to come later!
- ***Identify and clarify confusing ideas*** with tactful questions that will lead to better explanations. This will help you and your classmates better understand the material and will impress your instructor.
- ***Focus on the quality*** of your participation rather than the quantity.
- ***Keep your comments brief*** and to the point.
- ***Make relevant links to past class experience*** or current events to demonstrate your thorough understanding of the information.
- ***Try to answer a question,*** even if you are not sure of the answer.

Developing your answer will help you understand how the correct answer should be formulated.

- ***Be courageous*** enough to tactfully and thoughtfully disagree with a statement made during class. This can make class more interesting and lead to deeper understanding of the material.

Don't:

- ***Verbally attack an instructor*** or classmate if you disagree with their comments or opinions.
- ***Use profanity*** or other forms of offensive language.
- ***Interrupt your instructors*** or classmates.
- ***Dominate class discussions.***
- ***Forget to be respectful*** and courteous at all times.

Do you know how to take notes? Most college students would answer yes, of course they do. But, do you really know how to take notes?

If you're not sure, then reading this chapter will be an extremely valuable investment. Why? Taking good notes is an essential tool of your study program, and will be the key to a successful learning experience.

This chapter will help you become a successful note taker by:

- Helping you understand why taking notes is an important part of learning.
- Describing how to take effective lecture notes.
- Describing how to take effective notes from your textbooks.
- Outlining effective strategies for using your notes as part of an effective study program.

Why Take Notes?

There's no doubt about it – taking notes can be tedious. Sometimes, it may even seem that note taking is redundant and a waste of time. But note taking is important because it aids in the learning process. Taking notes will:

- ***Strengthen your listening skills.*** To take good notes, you will have to practice active listening in order to process the information.

- ***Reinforce the information*** so that you can truly learn it and recall it.
- ***Develop a written guide*** and a visual aid to assist you as you study.
- ***Make studying easier.***

Taking Lecture Notes

Of course, some of the most important information you will learn – and much of what will be included on exams – will be imparted by your instructor during lectures. Good instructors don't just regurgitate information already included in textbooks and other class materials – they build on basic knowledge, clarify points, raise questions and discuss viewpoints that add depth and value to what you read. Taking good notes during lectures is essential. To take good notes, follow these tips:

Prepare, Prepare, Prepare
As with most things, preparation is half the battle. Attending a lecture prepared will help you develop a better understanding of the information being presented and will make note taking much easier and effective. To prepare for a lecture:

- ***Complete all reading and homework assignments.*** Instructors have a rhyme a reason when they give you assignments. Most assignments familiarize students with information that will be covered in class in more detail and with more depth. If you are already familiar with the concepts being covered, you will spend less time trying to catch up and more time taking effective notes that will help you truly learn.
- ***Review your notes*** from previous lectures. This will help you understand the material and develop questions you might want to ask the instructor.
- ***Be on time to class.*** Many instructors begin their lectures by addressing student questions or concerns and reviewing or summarizing information from the previous lecture. The first few minutes of class are often the most important.
- ***Have the right supplies.*** Spend a few moments before each class making sure you have what you need to take notes. Some supplies you might need include your notebook, your textbook, a pen, pencil or highlighter, previous lecture notes and any other supplies that make you feel comfortable and prepared to take notes.
- ***Sit at the front your classrooms*** so you can see and hear your instructors clearly – including the body language and voice inflection they use to punctuate important points. You'll also be able to see what is written on the board or overhead better.

Listen, Learn And Then Take Notes

If you spend all your time writing, and none of it listening and absorbing the information presented by your instructor, the questions posed by your classmates and the discussions that arise during class, then you are defeating the purpose of being in class at all. And, if you don't listen during class, chances are your notes will make almost no sense to you by the time you get home. It takes a little practice, but make sure you listen to what is being said, comprehend the information, and then write a summary of what you have learned in your notes to help you recall the information at a later date.

Abbreviate

Abbreviating common terms or words that are repeated often during lectures will speed up the note taking process – and save your writing hand from overuse. Develop your own system of abbreviations for specific classes and become familiar with some basic shorthand. Some abbreviations for common words include:

w/	with
w/o	without
=	equals
Eg	for example
Esp	especially
c/w	compared with
!!	important
n.g.	no good
c/o	care of
~	approximately
b/c	because

Develop A Format That Works For You

Every student is different, and every student will take notes in a different way. It doesn't really matter exactly how you take notes, as long as you find the method that works for you and helps you succeed in your classes. Here are a few things to consider as you develop your own note taking style:

- ***Write clearly.*** This is a no-brainer – if you can't read what you write, your notes will be useless.
- ***Worry about mistakes later.*** You won't spell everything correctly or always use perfect grammar, but don't dwell on it while you are taking notes. Cross out errors if necessary and fix your mistakes later. The important

thing is that you record important points and create a record of the lecture that will help you study later.

- ***Use a loose-leaf notebook*** instead of a spiral notebook. Loose-leaf notebooks give you the flexibility to re-arrange the order of your notes and add additional pages.
- ***Leave a two-inch margin on the left-hand side of your paper.*** You can even draw a line to mark this margin. Write your notes on the right-hand side of the page, leaving the margin on the left-hand side for supplemental information like key words, phrases and questions or ideas you might have.
- ***Leave space after every topic*** to add additional information later. This space will also physically mark changes in topics, making your notes easier to read and review later.
- ***Write notes in outline format,*** listing the primary topic and identifying details and supporting information beneath.
- ***Don't take notes on the backside of the paper.*** Writing only on one side makes the notes easier to read and review.

Search For Exam Clues

Most instructors actually give you the answers to exam questions during their lectures. If you know what clues to look for during lectures, you can identify potential exam questions and answers. Look for and mark these clues in your notes:

- ***Repetition of points,*** changes in voice inflection and enumerations of a series of points.
- ***Comparisons between items.***
- ***Anything written on a board,*** overhead or in a PowerPoint presentation.
- ***A sense of excitement or emphasis*** from the instructor as he/she conveys information.

Have A Plan If You Miss A Lecture

Occasionally you might miss a lecture. First, see if you can attend another session of the same class or view a videotaped version of the class that might be on file at the library or through your instructor. If these options are not available, speak with your instructor. If you have a legitimate excuse for missing the class, your instructor may share his lecture outline with you or give you an overview of the important points that were covered. In addition to speaking with your instructor, ask a reliable classmate if you can view their notes from the class, keeping in mind that everyone has a different style of taking notes and you will have to develop your own version of the class notes in order to structure the information in a way that is best for you.

Don't Give Up If Your Instructor Is Hard To Follow

Even instructors aren't perfect, and from time to time you may find that an instructor speaks very quickly or has an accent that makes it difficult for you to comprehend and take good notes. If this happens to you:

- ***Compare notes with classmates*** after each lecture to make sure that you are taking notes on the main points of the lecture and to help fill in what you may have missed.
- ***Consider using a recording device*** – after getting your instructor's permission first, of course.
- ***Meet with your instructor*** throughout the term to review materials and ask questions.
- ***Ask questions*** during the lecture. This can help to slow down an instructor who speaks too quickly, and will help clarify information.
- ***Ask your instructor to implement visuals*** during lectures, such as outlines or bulleted lists of key terms or points.

Taking Notes From Your Textbooks

So, you read your textbooks and class materials. Is that enough? Probably not. To really be a successful student, you should take notes on your reading assignments. Taking excessive notes is not necessary, but you do need to develop a good understanding of your reading so you can further develop that understanding during lectures. Here's how:

Read First, Then Take Notes

Many students think that they should take notes as they read. This is a mistake. During lectures you should listen, comprehend and then take notes. While reading, you should do much the same – read, comprehend and then take notes.

Choose The Right Time, Place And Schedule

You can probably think of thousands of things you would rather do than read a textbook. That is why it is essential for you to schedule time to read and take notes from your textbook. Consider the time and place you will do your reading very carefully and develop some strategies to help maintain concentration and a positive attitude. Here's how:

- ***Schedule time*** to read your textbook when you are the most alert and aware, like in the morning, after a workout, or between classes.
- ***If you must read your textbook at night, don't read in your dorm room or in bed*** – you'll just become distracted or fall asleep! Go to an area that is conducive to reading, like the library.

- ***Break up your reading periods*** into relatively small, manageable blocks of time.
- ***Don't read when you are hungry,*** tired, upset or bored.
- ***Keep a positive attitude*** by rewarding yourself after reading. Tell yourself that if you read for one hour, afterward you can then talk on the phone, watch TV or do another activity that you enjoy.

Review Before You Read
Don't jump into reading your textbook without a clue as to what you'll be reading. Most textbooks provide a list or outline of the important information that will be covered in each chapter. Review these lists or outlines so you can better process the information as you read.

Find The Main Points
Textbooks are written in a predictable format that provides a sequential order that supports facts and information that lead to a main point. Make sure you identify and understand these points as you read. But remember that knowing the main point is only one part of the process – when you understand how and why the main point was reached is when you truly understand and have learned.

Create A Formula And Definitions Sheet Or Note Cards
In many classes you will have to memorize formulas and/or definitions to succeed. You can highlight these formulas and definitions in your textbook and refer to them later. However, a better strategy is to create a separate, one-page sheet for all the formulas and definitions you must memorize. Even better, develop note cards that you can use to test yourself.

Highlight
Highlighters are great tools for calling attention to certain points. That said, many college students are infamous for their overuse of highlighters. Don't highlight the entire textbook – it defeats the purpose. Highlight only key points that you will need to locate later.

Develop A Summary
Many college students bring their textbooks to class and refer to points they have highlighted during the lecture to help them understand and take lecture notes. This is fine; however, a better method is to develop a one-page summary of your reading. This summary can be referred to quickly during class, and developing this summary is a great way to help you process and understand the information you have read.

How to Use the Notes You Take

After you have attended a lecture, it is time to develop your lecture and textbook notes into an effective study tool. Here's how:

Review And Compare
As soon as possible after the lecture, review your notes with the purpose of adding to or deepening the notes where necessary. Doing it sooner rather than later will help you recall information while it is still fresh in your mind. Now is the time to use the margins and spaces you left in your lecture notes to add information, make note of ideas or questions and clarify anything in your notes you find questionable. Meeting with some classmates after each lecture to compare notes is also a great strategy to help you fill in content you may have missed or areas that may need to be clarified.

Edit
Before your next class, edit your notes, using textbook notes, homework assignments and other information you may have gained from study groups, tutors or reading that will help you understand the content. While editing, make note of areas you are unclear on and create questions to ask about them during your next lecture. You may also find that you need to make a one-on-one appointment with your instructor to ask for help.

Rewrite
After reviewing, comparing and editing your notes, they may seem messy and cluttered. In this case, you should take the time to rewrite your notes. This will not only create a more organized and clear version of your notes, it will help you to review and absorb the information better. When rewriting, use the same format and continue to leave spaces and margins in case more information becomes available later.

Organize
After you have finished developing a final version of your notes, you will need to organize them so you can effectively use them as a study tool for assignments and exams. Using a three-ring binder is a great way to organize notes, along with assignments, handouts and exams. Always date your notes by the date of the lecture to which they refer. That way if your notes get out of order or if you miss a lecture, you will easily be able to identify and order your notes quickly and correctly.

Review Your Process
After homework assignments or exams, review your notes to see how well you did recording information and identifying main points that were relevant to the homework and exams. Look at both the questions on which you did well and the questions on which you could have done better, and evaluate where your notes were effective and where you can improve. Then

develop strategies for taking notes that will serve as an even better study tool the next time.

Request Assistance

If you are unsure if you are taking good notes, make an appointment with your instructor and ask if he/she can take a look at your notes and give you advice on how to better record and organize the material that is important.

Protect

After all the hard work you have put into your notes, the last thing you want to do is lose them. You should take a few precautions to make sure that your notes are there when you need them:

- ***Rewrite the final version of your notes on a computer,*** then save the notes on the hard drive and on CD. Rewriting them one more time on the computer also will help you review the information, and will ensure that you have several versions of your notes – handwritten, computer hard drive and CD – for safekeeping.
- ***Make photocopies of your notes*** and store them in a safe place.
- ***Never lend the only copy of your notes*** to a classmate – lend photocopies instead.

Every student studies in a different way. Some students wake-up at the crack of dawn and study for hours before they start their day. Others study until very late at night. Many students find that the library is the ideal study environment. Other students study in unusual locations like a picnic table in the park, at the laundromat, or in their parents' dining room. One student may need to study for 20 hours a week, while another can get away with just 12 hours. There are as many study methods as there are students, but one thing is the same no matter what – every student must study to succeed in college.

This chapter will help you develop a study program that works for you by:

- Explaining when, where and how much you should study.
- Outlining the resources available to help you study.
- Recommending strategies and tips for effective and efficient studying.

When, Where and How Much?

When Should You Study?

The answer to this question is different for every person. However, the key to a successful study program is flexibility, commitment and effective time management. You should ask yourself when you are most likely to be dedicated and able to learn, how much you feel you need to study to be successful, and where in your busy schedule studying will best fit. Answer these questions and you will have the basic information you need to begin developing a study schedule that works for you.

Where Should You Study?

Again, not every location will fit every student. Libraries are often a good place to study – they are quiet, full of resources like computers and books, and facilitate concentration and learning. Many students try to study in their bedrooms, which is not always a good choice. Your bedroom has too many distractions – a ringing phone, a television and a comfy bed that encourages you to sleep!

Keep in mind that a good study location is:

- ***Convenient*** – not too far away, difficult to get to, or crowded.
- ***Comfortable*** – a comfortable temperature and good lighting.
- ***Quiet*** and conducive to activity and concentration, like a desk – not a bed.
- ***Free of distractions*** like telephones, TVs or radios. Even a high traffic area or a room with a good view can be distracting.
- ***Clutter-free.***

How Much Do You Need To Study To Be Successful?

Only you can answer this question. You will probably find that each of your classes requires a different amount of study time. For example, if you love English and it comes easy to you, but hate math, you may have to spend less time studying for your literature class and more time studying for calculus. A good rule of thumb as you begin your study program is to schedule two hours of study time for every hour that you spend in class. As the term progresses, you can make adjustments to your study schedule – spending more time on some areas, less on others.

Getting Help

When it comes to studying, you are not alone. You have a variety of resources that can help you study effectively and efficiently.

Study Groups

Studying is not always a solo effort. Studying with a group of fellow students can benefit you in many ways. Study groups can give participants a gauge by which to judge how well they understand the subject matter, an opportunity to clarify areas they are unsure of with other students, a sounding board off which to bounce views and perspectives, and the ability to share class notes, quiz each other and develop studying strategies. If you are interested in starting or joining a study group, do the following:

- ***Remember that to be effective, all members of the study group must be committed to learning,*** not just socializing.

- ***Find other students who are interested in learning more about the course*** by posting a notice on a public board or through word of mouth.
- ***Try to develop your study group with people who have diverse backgrounds and strengths*** to bring a wide range of perspectives and abilities to the group.
- ***Make sure participants have the time,*** desire and ability to meet on a regular basis.
- ***Develop ground rules*** so that everyone knows what is expected from each other. Making a timeline of what will be studied at each meeting is a good place to start.

Review Sessions

Many instructors offer review sessions before exams. During these sessions an instructor may provide a summary of highlights from class lectures, offer insights on the format and content of the exam, as well as answer questions that students may have. Don't miss these important sessions!

Instructors

A good relationship with your instructors is an important building block of a successful study program. Instructors know better than anyone how you should study for their classes, and most are willing to recommend strategies, tips and changes you can make to succeed. Visit with your instructors regularly and ask questions.

Tutors

Some colleges offer tutoring services at no charge. If your college offers this great resource, take advantage of it. If your college does not have a tutoring center, ask your academic advisor if he/she can recommend a good tutor, and investigate whether paying for a few sessions with a tutor is worth the investment.

Study On How To Study

If you find that your study skills are lacking across the board, it may be a good idea to take a class that teaches you how to study. Some colleges offer these classes at little or no cost. If your college does not offer these classes, look into local learning centers and professional test-preparation companies.

Tips for Success

Not every student will study in the same way, but there are a few strategies that seem to work for just about everyone. Aside from planning to study for an adequate amount of time, a great place to study and the right goals for you study time, you should also keep the following in mind to make sure the time you spend studying is spent well:

Attend Class
To study, you need to have the proper material. The best way to get this material is to attend lectures. Attending class gives you the opportunity to ask questions, discuss ideas and listen to the content firsthand. Perfect attendance is the best way to put your study habits on a course for success. Also, taking a few minutes after every class to review the material you just learned while it is still fresh in your mind is a great way to get your studying on the right track.

Be Consistent
Waiting until you absolutely have to study for a quiz or exam isn't the best choice. A better strategy is to maintain a regular study time throughout the term, so you can spread out your learning into manageable blocks of time. Studying for shorter periods daily will help you learn better than studying for hours on end just a day or so before the exams.

Know What You Are Studying For
Sure, you're studying for an exam, but what kind of exam? Will the questions be true/false, multiple choice or short essay? Will spelling and grammar count? How much time do you have to complete it? Finding out the answers to these kinds of questions will help you craft your study strategy. Some instructors will give you detailed information about exactly what format their exams will use. Others only give clues through their lectures, assignments and class materials. If, for example, an instructor is particularly fond of assigning short essays, you can bet short essays will appear on the exam, and you can study accordingly – by making sure you can write coherently and in detail about the ideas, theories and issues covered in the class. If, on the other hand, an instructor indicates that his/her exam will be all multiple choice, you might do better to study more content in less detail, paying special attention to definitions, dates and other factual information.

Learn From The Past
The best way to predict the content and format of an exam is to review the content of prior quizzes, assignments and exams. Visit with other students who have taken the course and instructor to see if they can give you advice on how to best prepare for exams given by your instructor. Also, keep all quizzes and exams so you can refer back to them – many final exams are cumulative and may include content and questions from prior quizzes and exams.

Set Goals
When you sit down to study, know what you want to accomplish. Reading for the next lecture, reviewing the previous day's notes or creating a timeline for studying for the final exam are all good goals. Setting goals will help you break your studying into manageable blocks and keep you from feeling overwhelmed.

Know Yourself

It may sound funny, but you really need to know yourself to study well. Understanding when you are most alert and likely to be dedicated to studying is an important part of developing a successful study program. If you are a morning person, you should study in the morning. Night owls should study at night. If you have a short attention span, schedule short study blocks. If you know that you are likely to skip study sessions scheduled during your favorite TV show or when your family meets for dinner on Sundays, then adjust your schedule accordingly. Before developing a study program and scheduling study time, ask yourself some difficult questions and take a good, hard look at your life and what is important to you. To be successful, your study program should fit into your life and priorities, not compete with them.

Focus On The Big Picture

Classes are taught in steps that should lead to an overall understanding of an issue or concept, and possibly the ability to perform certain functions or skills. For example, during a 19th-century literature class, you will read and discuss a series of novels, short stories and poems from that period. While you will have to grasp the meaning of each individual work of literature, the ultimate goal of the course is to help you develop a deeper understanding of that period in history and how the literature reflects that time. Focusing on what the ultimate goal of the course is – the big picture – will help you study more effectively for the course.

Take Advantage Of Every Minute

You can find time to study during any time of the day, if you try. Think about the downtimes in your day where you might be able to fit in a little studying. Have a two-hour break between classes? Studying at this time is a great idea – and your college most likely offers a lot of on-campus locations where you can study. Do you ride the bus or train or carpool to class? Are there downtimes at your part-time job where you are just sitting and your employer might not mind if you study?

With college comes the pressure to succeed. And with academic success comes pride and satisfaction in a job well done. Unfortunately, according to the Center for Academic Integrity, one-third of college students admit to serious cheating on exams, and one-half admit to serious cheating on a written assignment at least once.

True success can only come through academic honesty. However, students sometimes feel tempted to cheat, and believe that it is acceptable because:

- ***They see other students cheating.***
- ***They feel pressured to succeed*** by parents, friends or instructors.
- ***They fall behind*** or are unprepared for class assignments.
- ***They are pressured by other students*** or friends who need their help to cheat.
- ***They need to maintain a high grade-point average*** to keep financial aid or to enter graduate school.

This chapter will help you avoid the pressure to cheat, as well as maintain your academic honesty by:

- Defining cheating.
- Describing the consequences of cheating.
- Explaining how you can maintain academic honesty.

Defining Cheating

When you think of cheating, you probably think of a student copying answers off a classmate. But most colleges have a much broader range of behaviors that can be defined as cheating. Cheating also includes:

- ***Plagiarizing,*** or copying passages, sentences or ideas from a book, article or Internet Web site.
- ***Letting someone else complete your class work for you.***
- ***Using restricted materials*** during an exam, such as notes or books.
- ***Arranging for someone else to take an exam for you.***
- ***Communicating with other students during exams*** – either by speaking, giving or receiving signals, or exchanging written information.
- ***Receiving the content of an exam*** prior to the exam date.
- ***Storing information to assist you during an exam*** on an electronic device, like a scientific calculator.
- ***Not following the instructions*** given to you by an instructor on how to complete an assignment or exam.
- ***Not reporting another student's cheating.***

If any student participates in the above activities, they can be accused of cheating and may have to face serious consequences.

Consequences of Cheating

Every college deals with issues of academic honesty in different ways. Be sure that you know and understand your own school's policies regarding academic honesty and cheating to avoid being accused of cheating.

Cheating is rarely ignored in a college setting, and nearly always comes with consequences. A student who is caught cheating may:

- ***Be reprimanded by the instructor*** by being given a lower grade, or even a failing grade, in the class.
- ***Be reported to the college's administration.*** Many colleges require instructors to report students who are caught cheating.
- ***Face a hearing*** where he or she will have to defend themselves to a panel of instructors, administrators and students.
- ***Receive a failing grade*** for the course, be suspended from college, or even expelled.

- ***Have difficulty transferring*** to a different college or pursuing an advanced degree if the incidence of cheating is made part of his or her permanent academic record.
- ***Forfeit tuition*** or lose scholarship funding.
- ***Face stress and embarrassment*** as a result of his or her loss of an education.
- ***Find that they can be caught and punished for cheating long after the incident.*** In fact, in one case a professor who received a tip and found that many of his students had cheated on term papers over the past several semesters had many of these students expelled and some of the students' degrees revoked.

Of course, the biggest consequence of cheating is that you lose the opportunity to truly learn. It may be a cliché, but when students cheat they really are cheating themselves.

Maintaining Your Academic Honesty

College isn't easy. It takes a lot of dedication, commitment and hard work. Maintaining your academic honesty won't always be easy, especially when you have two exams, a term paper and a final project due on the same day. However, the benefits of maintaining your academic honesty far outweigh the consequences of cheating.

To Maintain Your Academic Honesty At All Times, Be Sure To:

- ***Understand that successfully completing your courses will take hard work,*** preparation and time management.
- ***Discuss difficult situations with your instructor,*** who may help you develop a plan to succeed in the course.
- ***Request assistance from your academic advisor*** or college counseling service.
- ***Take advantage of your school's tutoring center,*** ask friends to tutor you, or hire a personal tutor, like a graduate student, to help you master the content of the course.
- ***Join or coordinate a study group.***
- ***Report cheaters*** to your instructor if you know that students are cheating.

It's inevitable – someday, probably soon, you will have to take a college exam. Of course, taking exams is probably not your favorite pastime, but exams are important for many reasons.

First of all, exams give students an incentive to learn class material. Truth be told, even some of the best students probably wouldn't be highly motivated to attend class, study and learn if they knew they would never be tested on their ability to do so. Exams also provide students with an opportunity to test their own abilities and progress, allowing them to identify gaps in their knowledge and evaluate how their performance compares to their peers. Instructors use exams too, to both gauge their students' progress and to evaluate their own teaching strengths and weaknesses. If, for example, an entire class performs poorly on one section of an exam, it indicates to an instructor that he/she did not teach that area of the material very well and it needs to be covered again.

While exams do measure your performance in a specific academic area, they do not measure your intelligence, commitment or value as a person. Sometimes students who attend class, study hard and dedicate themselves to doing well in a course still perform poorly on exams. Anxiety, weak test-taking skills, even a bad mood can all affect a person's ability to ace an exam – even if they know the material.

Don't get tripped up by the pitfalls of test taking. There are steps you can take to make sure you develop the kinds of skills you need to take exams successfully.

This chapter will show you how by:

- Explaining the types of exams you are likely to encounter in college.
- Recommending some test-taking strategies.
- Outlining what you should do after each exam.

Types of College Exams

As if the idea of an exam wasn't stressful enough, you also need to know that there are a variety of exam types that you are likely to encounter during your college career. The following is a run-down of the most common exam types and how to deal with them. Also, keep in mind that many college exams will be a combination of a few or even all of these kinds of exams – an exam with ten true/false questions, ten multiple choice questions, and two essay questions, for example.

Essay Exams

An essay exam asks you to answer one or more questions in essay form. You will need to organize your thoughts and ideas into several paragraphs. Essay exams are graded subjectively – meaning that your grade is based on your instructor's opinion of how well you answered the questions – but there will be certain facts and concepts you will be expected to demonstrate your understanding of in the answer. Students who do not do well on essay exams often fail to answer the questions fully, and don't organize their answers well. When taking essay exams remember to:

- ***Read each of the questions*** carefully before starting and make sure you understand them fully. Then answer the questions you are most confident about first.
- ***Outline your thoughts*** and key points before you begin writing.
- ***Budget your time wisely,*** paying attention to how much each question is worth and dividing your time accordingly.
- ***Write legibly*** – your instructor has to be able to read your answer to grade it.
- ***Include as much relevant information in your answers as possible.***
- ***Leave some space at the end of your answers*** in case you want to add information later.
- ***Make your answer as specific*** as possible and avoid generalities. Experienced instructors can easily spot an answer that is long on words but short on substance from a mile away.

- ***Develop a summary sentence*** at the beginning of your essay. Then go on to further develop the ideas you have summarized. If you run out of time and aren't able to develop your answer further, at least you have demonstrated that you have basic knowledge of the subject. This can often be worth at least partial credit.
- ***Take a shortcut if you run out of time.*** If you find yourself short of time on a question, skip writing a complete essay and just outline key points of your answer. Although you will probably lose credit because your answer is not in essay form, your instructor may give you partial credit because you have demonstrated that you understand the question and know the answer.
- ***Check your answers*** quickly for spelling and grammar mistakes.

True/False Exams

A true/false test is a test where you are given statements and must judge whether they are true (*right*) or false (*wrong*). When taking true/false exams, remember to:

- ***Read all of the statements before you begin.*** Then answer the questions you know the answers to first. Answering these questions may help you develop the answers to other questions you are less sure of.
- ***Carefully consider statements in a "negative" format.*** Some instructors will use negatives to confuse you. For example:

  It is not always true that all birds use their wings to fly.

  All birds use their wings to fly.

The answer to both of these questions is "false," but the first one is written in a negative format, making it more confusing. Pay attention to these kinds of questions and consider carefully before answering.

- ***Make sure every part of a statement is correct before deeming it "true."*** If any part of a statement is incorrect, the entire statement is false.
- ***Watch for words like "all," "most," "sometimes," "never," or "rarely."*** Adding words like these to a correct statement can change the meaning altogether, making it false.
- ***Take note if you have to provide an explanation to make a statement true.*** If you have to explain why it is true, then it is false.

Multiple-Choice Exams

A multiple-choice exam is an exam that presents you with a question and a list of possible answers from which you must choose the correct one. When taking a multiple choice exam remember to:

- ***Read all of the questions*** carefully before beginning the exam. Then, answer the questions you know the answers to first. Answering the questions you know first may help you gather information to help you answer questions you are less sure of.
- ***Try to think of the answer before looking at the list of choices.*** This will help you choose the right answer from a list of answers that may be very similar.
- ***Read over all of the possible answers*** and cross out the ones you are certain are incorrect and choose your answer from the choices that remain.
- ***Decline to answer, if necessary.*** Some instructors not only give no credit for incorrect answers, but also penalize for incorrect answers. In this case, it may not be worth the risk to answer questions you are not absolutely sure of.

Open Book Exams

Open book exams are exams where instructors allow students to use a list of pre-approved materials during the exam, including class notes and textbooks. Most students believe that open book exams are the easiest kind of exams because you are allowed to have access to your books and notes while taking the exam. Unfortunately, this is not true. Open book tests are often the hardest exams to take, for a few reasons. First, when students hear "open book exam," they often do not prepare well for the exam because they think that since they will have access to the information they need, they don't need to study. Students also waste time during open book exams using their materials to confirm the answers to questions they already know the answers to. Lastly, open book exams are often created to be more difficult and graded with higher standards because instructors are allowing students to use books and notes. When taking an open-book exam, remember to:

- ***Study just as you would for an exam*** that does not allow you access to your study materials.
- ***Tab and highlight pages*** and areas in your textbook and notes you think you will need easy access to during the exam, particularly material that you find difficult. That way you won't waste time tracking down this information during the exam.
- ***Read all of the questions carefully*** before beginning the exam. Then answer the questions you are sure of – without confirming your answers in your materials. If you have time at the end of the exam, then you can confirm these answers.
- ***Develop your answers first,*** then use your materials to confirm or expand your answers.
- ***Cite your materials whenever possible*** and where appropriate.

- ***Leave space as you develop your answers.*** If you have time later to expand your answers using information found in your materials, you will have room to write more.

Take-Home Exams

Take-home exams are exams that you are allowed to take home to complete. If this sounds like a dream come true, you should remember that take-home exams come with many of the same perils as open-book exams. Because students know they will be able to bring the exam home to complete, they may not study for it. Instructors often design take-home exams to be very challenging, and may have much higher grading standards. Procrastination, distractions and poor time management can also cause students to perform poorly on take-home exams. If you are taking a take-home exam, remember to:

- ***Study just as you would for any other exam.***
- ***Choose the right environment in which to take your exam*** – quiet, free of distractions and uncluttered. Just because you are taking the exam at home doesn't mean you should take it in front of the TV or while talking on the phone.
- ***Organize your study materials,*** including notes, reading and homework assignments in advance of the exam.
- ***Review the exam before leaving the classroom*** to see if you have any questions about the exam. Also, ask your instructor if you are allowed to contact him/her with questions and how he/she would prefer to be contacted.
- ***Take this kind of exam the same as any other*** – answering the questions you are sure of first, then moving on to the more difficult questions.
- ***Be sure you develop strong and thorough answers.*** Remember – instructors have higher standards when they grade take-home exams.
- ***Use a word processing program*** to answer questions, if possible. If this is not an option, be sure to write legibly.
- ***Cite materials when possible.***

Oral Exams

Oral exams are exams where you are expected to answer orally, instead of by writing answers to the questions. Oral exams are more common during graduate school, but you may find an occasion when you will have to take an oral exam, especially if you are taking foreign language classes. When taking oral exams, remember to:

- ***Meet with your instructor*** to find out how the oral exam will be conducted.

- ***Prepare for the exam*** by conducting mock exams with a classmate.
- ***Dress and act appropriately during the exam.***
- ***Arrive early to the exam*** so you can relax, focus and make a good impression on the instructor.
- ***Pause before answering*** to give yourself time to think out your answer. If you need more time, ask the instructor to repeat the question.
- ***Summarize your answer*** in your first sentence and then continue by developing the key points.
- ***Avoid rambling or using one-word answers.*** You are judged on how well you demonstrate your knowledge, not on how much you can say or how quickly you can answer.
- ***Try to avoid annoying speech mannerisms*** like "um" or "you know" or "like." Also avoid slang or language that appears disrespectful or unprofessional.

Exam Strategies

Everyone knows you have to study to prepare for an exam. But what else? While how well you study is a big predictor of how well you will do on an exam, there are many other things that are important to your performance. The following tips will help you cover all the bases as you prepare for your exams.

Take Care Of Yourself
You wouldn't stay up all night, eat junk food and pop caffeine pills the night before running a marathon, would you? Of course not. So why do it before an exam? Taking care of yourself in the days leading up to an important exam is one of the most important things you can do to ensure success. Remember to:

- ***Maintain a regular diet and sleep schedule.*** Eating junk food and skipping sleep can affect your performance.
- ***Exercise to reduce stress.*** Taking a study break for a quick workout can help you burn off stress and refocus.
- ***Take a shower to help you relax and focus.***
- ***Snack during exams if you're allowed.*** Bringing a small snack and bottle of water to a long exam can boost your energy.
- ***Don't rush.*** Oversleeping on the morning of an exam is not a good idea. The last thing you want is to feel stressed out and rushed as you are getting ready to leave for an exam. Organize yourself and pack your bag the night before and make sure you leave with plenty of time to spare.

Arrive Early
Get to your exam early so you can choose a comfortable place to sit, organize your materials and ask any last-minute questions you might have for your instructor.

Stay Positive
As you're sitting with your exam in front of you, take a deep breath and relax. Then visualize yourself doing well on the exam. Staying calm and keeping a positive attitude will boost your performance.

Be Comfortable
An exam is not the place to wear your tightest jeans and itchiest sweater. Dress in layers so you can take off or put on layers if you are too warm or too cold, and wear clothes you know are comfortable.

Preview The Exam
Before diving in, take time to familiarize yourself with the exam. Look over every section and determine how much time you should spend on each.

Follow Directions
Many costly mistakes have been made on exams simply because students did not read the directions. It may look like a straightforward essay test to you, but if you skip the instructions you will never know if you only have to answer only two out of the four questions.

Answer What You Know First
Students are always tempted to answer exam questions in order. This is a mistake. While previewing the exam, mark the questions you know the answers to, then complete these first. This strategy will help you get off to a positive start and ensure that you get to the questions you know before time runs out. You will also save as much time as possible to work on the more difficult questions.

Make It Easy For The Instructor
Your instructor quite possibly has hundreds of exams to grade in a very short period of time. What does this mean to you? It means that your instructor will not waste valuable time trying to decipher your bad handwriting or figuring out how you arrived at your answer. Write legibly and make sure you show your work, including any calculations or steps you performed to arrive at your answer. Sometimes, even when an answer is incorrect, an instructor might give partial credit if a student took the correct steps to figure out the problem.

Avoid Distractions
Distractions can mean the difference between doing okay on an exam and doing great. Avoid distractions at all costs. Don't sit next to fellow students who might distract you. Sit away from windows where the view might cause

you to lose your focus. Leave your loud-ticking watch at home. It's not always possible to anticipate all circumstances that can distract you, but do what you can to control your environment.

Don't Know? Don't Panic

It happens to the best of us – no matter how well you study, there will be a question or two that takes you by surprise. When this happens to you, don't panic. Skip the question and go on to the questions you do know the answers to. When it is time for you to answer the difficult question, use as much information as you can to develop your answer. Instructors sometimes give partial credit to students who demonstrate a degree of knowledge or understanding, even if they cannot answer the question correctly or completely.

Learn As You Go

Exam questions are usually related and may even build on one another. As a result, knowing the answer to one question may help you answer another question you are not as sure of. As always, answer the questions you are sure of first, then try to glean any clues from these questions that may help you with others.

Remember The Turn-In Checklist

Don't turn in an exam until you go through the checklist! Before turning in your exam, you should:

- ***Identify yourself.*** Make sure your name, student ID number and other required information are included.
- ***Review for success.*** Review the exam to make sure you answered all the questions and did everything you were asked to do. Also, check for spelling and grammar mistakes. If you used a Scantron or "bubble" answer sheet, make sure you filled in the correct bubble for each question.
- ***Turn it in on time!*** Some instructors will not accept exams even a minute late. However, don't be afraid to request additional time if you need it – it doesn't hurt to ask.

Cram – If You Must

It's not an ideal situation, but nearly all students find it necessary at one time or another. You may have an exam tomorrow, and you are not prepared. It's time to cram. When you must cram, remember to:

- ***Keep a positive attitude.*** This is not the time to get down on yourself or panic. If you attended class and completed assignments, you should be fine.

- ***Be efficient.*** Whatever time you have to study should be used as efficiently as possible. Concentrate on main points and unfamiliar information rather than reviewing what you already know.
- ***Take breaks*** and take care of yourself for maximum focus. Eat well, take time for walks and sneak in a cat nap if you can.
- ***Stay alert.*** Don't study on a bed or couch where you will most likely fall asleep.
- ***Skip the caffeine.*** Sodas, coffee and caffeine pills may keep you awake as you study late into the night, but how you will feel in the morning will affect your performance. The same goes for junk food!
- ***Rest.*** Try to squeeze in as much sleep as possible. Being well-rested will probably help you perform better than the amount of studying you would have been able to do in those late, late hours of the night.

Control Anxiety

It's normal to be anxious before an important exam. The key is controlling this anxiety before it affects your performance. If you are anxious, you should:

- ***Keep things in perspective.*** Of course, your grade on an exam is important, but just how important? It is highly unlikely that one grade on one exam in one class will affect or change your life in a big way. Remember: exams evaluate your knowledge of a specific area of information – they are not a judge of your value, your intelligence, or your ability to succeed in life. Performing poorly on an exam is not the end of the world. Simply remembering this can help you stay calm.
- ***Keep in touch with your instructor.*** Schedule time at least a week before the exam to meet with your instructor to ask questions and clarify anything you are not sure of.
- ***Take care of yourself.*** Don't let stress rule your life. Eat well, get enough sleep and exercise in the days leading up to your exam.
- ***Give yourself enough time to prepare.*** Feeling rushed as you study will add to your anxiety. If you think you need a week to study, schedule yourself ten days just to be sure.
- ***Get help.*** Join a study group or ask a fellow student to study with you. Having support will reassure you that you are prepared.
- ***Avoid quizzing yourself or cramming in the minutes before the exam.*** You are not likely to retain anything you learn in these last minutes, and it may cause doubt and stress.
- ***Visualize success!***

After the Exam

The exam is over. Breathe a sigh of relief! But your job is not over yet. In many ways, what you do after the exam is as important as what you do in preparation. After the exam, you should:

Reward Yourself

You've done a great job, so give yourself some credit. Try to schedule some time after your exam to relax and unwind. Splurge on an activity that you enjoy and give yourself time for a breather. That way you'll be re-energized for whatever lies ahead – and you'll have something to look forward to as you work hard preparing for your next exam.

Review Your Graded Exam

Many students take a look at the grade on the top, then file the exam away. Big mistake. Carefully reviewing your exam is important because it can help you catch mistakes your instructor may have made during the grading process, and it will help you understand the mistakes you made so you can correct them on future exams. When reviewing your exam:

- ***Make sure your grade has been calculated correctly.*** Sometimes a simple math mistake on the part of the grader can mean the difference between an "A" and a "B."
- ***Look for questions you feel were unclear*** or that could have been answered in more than one way. Then talk with your instructor about it to see if your answer could be considered correct.
- ***Figure out where the questions came from*** – from your textbook, assignments, lectures, etc. This will help you to pinpoint which materials are the most important to study on the next exam.
- ***Figure out the correct answers*** to questions you got wrong or received partially correct. Make note of where you made your mistakes and what information you were missing. This will help you learn from your mistakes so you can do better on the next exam.
- ***Schedule an appointment with your instructor*** to discuss the exam, if necessary.
- ***Look for patterns.*** If you find that you always do poorly on essay questions, maybe you need to take a writing seminar. If true/false questions always trip you up, perhaps you aren't reading the statements carefully enough and need to slow down. Always have several questions you leave unanswered because you run out of time? You might need to rethink your time management during exams. Evaluating your exams can help you identify strengths and weaknesses so you can develop a plan to improve.

As a new college student, you are probably already picturing the day you will receive your diploma. As a college graduate, you will have a world of opportunities available to you. But a college diploma may not be enough. In fact, some college graduates find that there is just one thing standing between them and the future of their dreams – their grades.

The grades you will receive in your college course work are more important than you might think. Graduate school admissions officers and employers both rely heavily on grade point averages and grades in specific areas of coursework to weed out the weak candidates and make choices about who they will admit and hire. While the most important thing you can get out of your college experience is a solid education, you should also be committed to earning the highest grades possible.

This chapter will help you earn the kind of grades that reflect your potential for success by:

- Helping you understand the grading process.
- Outlining alternative grading options available to you.
- Describing the value of starting your college career with good grades.
- Recommending strategies to receive and maintain good grades.

How are You Graded?

Taking tests and receiving grades is difficult for college students. What you might not realize is that evaluating student performance on class work and assigning grades is difficult for instructors, too! In fact, many college instructors name grading as the most difficult part of teaching.

Every instructor has a different method for evaluating student performance and computing grades. Some instructors may offer extra credit assignments. Other instructors may allow you to drop your lowest exam grade. Some instructors grade you on class participation, while others grade you only on written work. However, regardless of how instructors format their evaluation and grading, most colleges encourage instructors to create grading systems that follow a few basic criteria:

- ***Grades should accurately reflect a student's performance.***
- ***The grading system should be clear*** so that students can chart their progress in the class.
- ***The grading system should be fair.***

Most instructors rely on one of the two following grading systems, or some variation:

Absolute Grading
This is the most common grading system. With absolute grading, your instructor will set the percentage range for each letter grade, and all students whose performance falls within that range will receive the correlating grade. For example, the most common breakdown of grades is as follows: students who receive a 90-100% receive an A, 80-89% a B, 70-79% a C, 60-69% a D, and 59% or below a failing grade.

Relative Grading
Also known as "grading on a curve," this grading system has become more popular in recent years because it helps to correct course work problems that instructors might have – like tests or assignments that are too easy or too difficult. One way of looking at relative grading is to realize that you are being graded on your performance in relation to your classmates. In this system, your grade is based on the distance that your score is from the average score of the entire class. For example, if the average score of the class is 79%, your instructor will use a standard deviation calculation to determine the break-off points for each grade. In this case, 89-100% is an A, 85-88% is a B, 72-84% is a C, 60-71% is a D, and 59% or below is a failing grade.

Ultimately, it is your responsibility to know how your grades will be determined. To do this, you must first understand how your performance will be evaluated and how grades will be assigned. Be sure you understand the processes and systems that each of your instructors use. If you are unclear on grading criteria, or find that you are having difficulty tracking your progress in a class, make an appointment to speak with your instructor. Chances are, if you are having difficulty, other students are too, and your instructor needs to know.

Grading Options

In most of your classes you will complete work throughout the term and be assigned a final grade based on the merit of your work. However, sometimes circumstances require students to deviate from the typical grading process and take advantage of other options available to them. Some of these options include:

Pass/Fail
Many colleges give students the option of forgoing getting graded and allow them to receive either a "Pass" or "Fail" mark in a class. Usually this option is available only for non-required classes, or electives. This may be a good option for students who would like to explore other areas of interest but do not want their experimentation with new classes to affect their overall GPA. For example, if you would like to take a physical education class in golf, but are not sure how well you will perform, the pass/fail option may work for you. Keep in mind that your transcripts will indicate that you took the class with this option, and graduate school acceptance committees and employers may ask you to explain why you chose it.

Incomplete
Sometimes students encounter circumstances, such as a death in the family or a prolonged illness, that make them unable to complete a course within the standard time. In these cases, many colleges allow students additional time to complete the course work. Usually, students who choose this option must make arrangements with their instructor and successfully complete all required course work by a designated time. Until the course work is complete, an "Incomplete" will appear on the student's transcript. After the course work is completed, the earned grade will replace the Incomplete.

Drop/Add
Most colleges maintain a period of time after the term has started during which students can drop or add classes to their schedules. This allows students to go to the first meeting or two of a class and make an informed decision about whether they would like to continue in the class, replace it with another one, or drop the class altogether. Most colleges also allow students to drop a class at a later date in the term if they are doing poorly or other unforeseen circumstances have come up that will make it difficult for the student to successfully complete the class. Keep in mind that most colleges limit the time frame in which you can drop a class. If you wait too long, your college may keep some or all of the tuition you paid for

the dropped class. Dropping classes also may delay your progress toward graduation, so this option should be used as a last resort.

Challenging Your Grades

Even college instructors make mistakes. Sometimes students may find that an exam or assignment has been graded incorrectly, or that a question or assignment was worded improperly, leading to confusion and incorrect answers. Other times students may feel that an instructor has treated them and their work unfairly. If this happens to you:

- ***Gather the information you need*** to defend your belief that your grade is incorrect or unfair. Refer to class notes, textbooks, previous assignments and tests.
- ***Make an appointment*** to speak with your instructor to review the grade in question and present your concerns.
- ***If your instructor disagrees with your belief that the grade is incorrect or unfair, avoid defensiveness or anger.*** Listen to your instructor's reasoning carefully so that you fully understand the situation.
- ***If, after meeting with your instructor, you are still unsatisfied, you can present your argument to the department that oversees the course.*** Most colleges have a grade-petitioning process that allows you to appeal your grade to a department committee.
- ***If all else fails, speak with your academic advisor for help.***

The Value of Starting with Good Grades

Starting your college career with a good grade point average and maintaining good progress is a lot easier than digging yourself out of a hole. If you don't believe this, take a look at the following chart that tracks the progress of "Jack" and "Jill."

First Term	**Jack**	**Jill**
Chemistry (*4 credit hours*)	C	A
Anthropology (*3 credit hours*)	B	A
Creative Writing (*4 credit hours*)	C	A
Calculus (*4 credit hours*)	B	A
Grade Point Average	**2.47**	**4.0**

Second Term	Jack	Jill
Chemistry II (*4 credit hours*)	B	B
Art History (*3 credit hours*)	A	B
Biology (*4 credit hours*)	A	B
Calculus II (*4 credit hours*)	A	A
Grade Point Average	**3.73**	**3.27**
Cumulative Grade Point Average	**3.10**	**3.63**

As you can see from this example, Jack did poorly his first term. Fortunately for Jack, he realized his mistakes and took steps in his second term to correct them. Even so, he has a long way to go if he intends to raise his cumulative GPA, considering that his classes will only get more difficult.

Starting college with good grades is like an insurance policy: it protects you from potential GPA disaster if you get a lower grade later in your college career. If you don't have this insurance, you are not only risking your GPA, but also your future.

Some Strategies for Good Grades

Studying, attending class, completing course work and mastering a course's content are the keys to getting good grades. But there are some other things you should keep in mind as you earn your grades:

Do:

- ***Remember that your instructors are only human***, and may make mistakes. It is your responsibility to carefully check your work for correct grading, and to keep up with your grade point average to make sure that the grade you earn is the grade you receive. If you feel that an error has been made in your grade, bring it to your instructor's attention.
- ***Make sure you understand the criteria your performance will be judged by***, and the system your instructor will use to assign grades.
- ***Become familiar with the grading options*** that are available to you and make informed and thoughtful decisions about using these options.

Don't:

- ***Lose focus*** as you enjoy your experience as a new college student and think that your freshman-year grades don't matter because you can make up for them later.

- ***Get defensive or angry*** if you disagree with a grade you have received. Become familiar with how your college handles these kinds of situations and participate in the process.
- ***Give up.*** Any improvement you can make in your grades – either in a specific course during a term or in your overall grade point average – will help and is worth the effort.

Chapter 14

Achieving Success

Imagine what your life will look like when you are successful. Do you have plenty of money? A beautiful home? A wide circle of family and friends? Awards and honors on your wall?

Every person's vision of success is different. While one individual may define success by making a decent salary, living in a neighborhood with good schools and raising happy children, another individual may not feel successful until they have published a bestselling book or been voted into public office. Still others define success by meeting the perfect person to spend their life with. Some people feel successful if they simply wake up every day and feel happy.

The path to success is a very personal and individual journey, but there are some common denominators that will decide whether a person will be successful or not. The number one common denominator? Taking risks.

You've heard it a million times, but you really can't succeed if you don't try. Sounds easy enough, right? Then why do so many people still fail to succeed? And how do you ensure that you won't fail?

Because everyone's vision of success is unique, everyone's path to success will be different. It would be impossible to tell you how to achieve your own personal vision of success – only you can do that. But you can develop skills and characteristics that will prepare you for success.

This chapter will show you how by:

- Outlining the top reasons people fail – and how to avoid them.
- Explaining the pitfalls that students encounter on the journey to success.
- Recommending strategies to overcome your fears and pursue success.

The Top Ten Reasons People Fail

If you ask twenty people about their biggest failure, you will get twenty very different stories. Just as every person's personal vision of success is unique, every person's reasons for failing are unique as well. However, in people who continue to fail rather than succeed, you will most likely begin to see similarities in their personalities and approaches to life. People who fail to succeed:

1. **Have Poor People Skills**
   Underestimating the importance of good people skills is a big mistake. Everything we do requires us to interact with people, and the better we are able to do it, the more successful we will be. Developing strong and effective people skills is essential to your success.
2. **Have A Negative Attitude**
   If you have a bad attitude, it's hard to succeed. Your attitude should not be determined by circumstances, other people or the world around you. Your attitude must be determined by you. Develop a great attitude and learn how to make the best of even bad situations, and you are halfway to success.
3. **Fail To Set Goals**
   You can't succeed without a plan. Setting goals is how you structure your plan for success – one step at a time. Goals are also a great way to measure your progress, focus your efforts, develop confidence and pride in your abilities, and set the direction for your future.
4. **Resist Change**
   Ever heard the saying, "The only thing that remains constant is change?" Well, it's true. In your life you will find that people, circumstances, the world, even you, will change. Failing to adjust and adapt to changes is a surefire way to derail your success. When you know that a change needs to be made in your life, make it! Your success depends on it.
5. **Don't Prioritize**
   Even the most successful person in the world can't do everything well all at once – they set priorities for tasks, projects and goals that help them

achieve what is most important first. Setting priorities – both for short-term tasks and for long-term goals – is vital to every person's success.

6. Lack Commitment

People who are successful commit to their goals, the task at hand – and to themselves. That means not questioning your purpose, your talents and skills, or your value as a person. It also means following through on things that are important to you – from start to finish.

7. Are Inflexible

It's great to have a plan and stay the course. In fact, it's one of the ways you achieve success. But developing tunnel vision and becoming paralyzed when life deviates from your plan is a quick route to failure. Life is a crazy ride – up one minute, down the next, then a hairpin turn in the opposite direction! To be truly successful, you need to develop the kind of flexibility that allows you to take the twists and turns life throws you in stride – and turn them into assets.

8. Look For Shortcuts

It's only human – everyone wants an easy way to achieve their goals. That's why every other commercial on television is for diet pills, outlandish get-rich schemes and crazy exercise contraptions. Successful people don't buy into the idea that there is a shortcut to success. They understand that time, hard work and dedication are the only true routes to success.

9. Rely On Talent And Skill Alone

If you are blessed with talent and skill in a specific area, you are already ahead of the game. But you will fail to succeed if you believe that your special talents and skills guarantee your success. Even the most talented people have to put a lot of time and work into achieving success. For example, a kid might be born with a spectacular talent for baseball, but if he doesn't show up for Little League practice, doesn't get the good grades necessary to earn a place at a college with a good baseball team, and doesn't exercise and practice his talent on a regular basis, he might as well not have been born with any talent at all. Your talents and skills are unique and amazing – but it is up to you to take what you have been given and use it to achieve your own vision of success.

10. Don't Take Responsibility For Their Actions

Even successful people make mistakes – lots of them. The difference between successful people and unsuccessful people is that successful people don't blame others for their mistakes – they take responsibility for them. When you take responsibility for your actions, you earn people's respect and trust, you gain a true picture of your strengths and weaknesses, and you allow yourself to learn from your mistakes so you can avoid the same pitfalls in the future. On the other side of the coin, when you don't blame others and take responsibility for your actions, you are then fully able to take credit when things go well because of you!

Why Students Fail to Succeed

You now understand the personal characteristics that lead people away from success. But why do many college students fail to fulfill their true potential?

The reasons college students fail to succeed are not that different from the reasons people in general fail to succeed – they are just more specific to the goals of college students. Take a look at the following list of common traits of college students who fail to succeed, and see if you recognize any of these traits in yourself. Then take action to correct them.

College students who fail to succeed:

- ***Have weak study skills.***
- ***Have poor time management skills.***
- ***Fail to attend class regularly.***
- ***Don't prepare for class, assignments and exams.***
- ***Don't study correctly or enough.***
- ***Lack motivation and purpose.***
- ***Don't ask for help when they need it*** or take advantage of available resources.
- ***Don't establish personal goals.***
- ***Overextend themselves*** with extracurricular activities and other commitments.
- ***Don't adjust well*** to the new freedom and responsibility of college life.
- ***Don't challenge themselves*** or step outside of their comfort zone.

The Secrets of Successful People

The secrets of successful people really aren't secrets at all. In fact, the two big secrets to success are just common sense:

You Have To Take Risks
Some of the world's greatest success stories have a lot to say about risk. Here are just a few:

> *He who is not courageous enough to take risks will accomplish nothing in life.*
>
> — *Muhammad Ali, Legendary boxer*

If you don't risk anything you risk even more.

— Erica Jong, Bestselling author

Great deeds are usually produced at great risks.

— Herodotus, Ancient writer and philosopher

These great people knew the number one way to success: you have to take risks. The word "risk" sounds dangerous, but we're not talking about jumping off cliffs or passing trucks on two-lane highways at breakneck speeds. Those kinds of risks are reckless and just plain stupid. The kinds of risks we are talking about are the calculated risks you need to take to achieve success – and you actually get opportunities to take these important risks every day. For example:

- When questions are asked by instructors in your classes, do you raise your hand, despite the risk of being wrong?
- When you meet someone you like, do you ask them out on a date, even though you risk being turned down?
- Do you sign up for classes that are challenging and outside of your comfort zone, even though you risk not doing well?
- Do you express your opinion when you are out with your friends, even though you risk being ridiculed or thought of as different?

If you answered yes to these questions, then congratulations: you are well on your way to taking the kinds of calculated risks you need to be a success. If you answered no, then it might be time for you to evaluate why you don't take risks. Chances are, it's fear (*more on that in the next section*). It's also time for you to think about what you are missing out on by not taking risks. If you don't raise your hand, you won't ever be wrong – but you also won't earn the respect of your instructors and classmates, and you won't learn as much either. Not asking that person you like out helps you avoid rejection – but you'll also be spending a lot of Friday nights alone and lonely. Risks are just that – risky. But they also lead to the greatest things in life – including success.

You Must Overcome Your Fears

Easier said than done, right? Everyone is afraid of something – in fact, most people are afraid of more things than they'd care to count. What are you afraid of? People laughing at you if you fall on your face? Letting down your family and friends? Losing money, time, face? Finding out that you really aren't as good at what you love to do as you thought? These are all legitimate fears – and ones that have stopped the most successful dead in their tracks. But successful people develop strategies for understanding and facing their fears that help them move forward:

- ***Understand the costs and benefits.*** When you are afraid of taking action, ask yourself – what is the worst thing that will happen to me if I try this and fail? Next, ask yourself – what could I potentially gain if I succeed? For example, running for class president comes with a lot of worst-case scenarios. You could make a fool of yourself while giving a speech. You could trip in front of hundreds of people while walking up the steps for the debate. You could lose. Or you could win and do a horrible job. But in what ways could you succeed? You could give a moving and amazing speech that helps you develop confidence in your public speaking skills. You could do well in debates and raise some interesting issues that get people talking. You could win the election. You could be a class president that makes real changes that help students. It could lead to bigger and better things. Thinking about these things helps you gain perspective – and realize that perhaps your fears are nothing in comparison to what you might gain.
- ***Face your fears.*** Avoiding your fears is useless. Even if you avoid what you fear, it won't go away and you will be left unable to develop strategies to deal with your fears. Face your fears, develop an understanding of why you fear what you do, and develop ways to deal with your fears in positive way.
- ***Focus on the positive.*** Don't waste your time thinking about how things could go wrong and how your worst fears could become reality. Instead, focus on the skills and talents you possess that will help you succeed, and on the ways that things could turn out right.
- ***See success.*** It's an old trick, but visualizing yourself overcoming your fears and succeeding really does work. Visualize the steps you will take to achieve success and envision how it will feel when you finally accomplish your goal.
- ***Keep at it.*** Robert F. Kennedy once said, "Only those who dare to fail greatly can ever achieve greatly." Hardly anyone achieves success on the first try. Learn from your mistakes and keep at it – it's the only way you will succeed.
- ***Just jump.*** As the Nike slogan says, "Just Do It!" Thinking about how you will succeed and making a plan is important – but if you spend all your time thinking and planning and none of it doing, you will never succeed. Take the first step and just keep going!

Success is more attitude than aptitude. If you believe this is true, then the kind of attitude you have toward life is actually more important to your success and happiness than how smart you are, how much you know, or how many skills and talents you have. If this is true, then why are so many people still walking around with negative attitudes? Because they don't realize how much their attitude affects everything they do. Don't make this mistake. Now that you know how important a positive attitude is, make sure you have one!

This chapter will show you how by:

- Explaining what a positive attitude is.
- Recommending strategies for creating a positive attitude.
- Outlining ways to maintain a positive attitude.

What is a Positive Attitude?

When someone has a positive attitude, you can feel it. Energy seems to radiate from them, and the feeling is contagious. It's difficult to pinpoint just what separates the positive people from the rest, but here are a few things that positive people have in common:

- ***Optimism*** – Positive people view the glass as half full, not half empty.
- ***Enthusiasm and Energy*** – Positive people are enthusiastic about life and live each moment to the fullest.
- ***Curiosity*** – Positive people are curious about the world and are driven by the desire to learn.

- ***Creativity*** – Positive people have the ability to think outside the box, view things differently and find new and better solutions.
- ***Confidence*** – Positive people have high self-esteem and are confident in their abilities.
- ***Resourcefulness*** – Positive people don't dwell on a problem, they find a solution.
- ***Productivity*** – Positive people manage their time, energy and efforts for maximum results – and are more productive because of it.
- ***Vision*** – Positive people can see beyond difficult situations to envision the possibilities. They also can see the best in things – and in people.
- ***Sense of Purpose and Direction*** – Positive people feel they have a purpose in life and know where they are going.
- ***Satisfaction*** – Positive people are satisfied with their efforts and with life in general.
- ***Strong Relationships*** – Positive people know that the key to a happy life is great relationships with family, friends and neighbors.
- ***Health*** – Positive people take steps to lead a healthy lifestyle.

Get Positive in 10 Steps

Some students admit they have a negative attitude, but believe there's not much they can do about it. "I'm a born pessimist," some may say. While it's true that some people are born naturally more positive than others, everyone can develop a positive attitude with a little effort. Try these simple steps to give your attitude a makeover:

1. **Give Yourself A Dose Of Perspective**
   You get a bad grade on a test, you are in a fight with your roommate, and your student loan check is two weeks late. It's hard to be positive when things aren't going your way. But before you resign yourself to negativity, take a deep breath and put things in perspective. It's highly unlikely that one bad grade on a test will ruin your entire college career. You have plenty of opportunities to improve your grades in the future. You're roommate won't be mad at you forever – in fact, a disagreement may actually help you learn more about each other and how to communicate better. And your student loan check will come eventually – the bill collectors will just have to wait. Even when things seem bad, a healthy dose of perspective can help you keep a positive outlook. You still have your health, your friends and a great life ahead of you. Remember that and you have no reason to be anything but positive.

2. **Be Confident**
Remembering that you have the ability to achieve anything you put your mind to is essential to maintaining a positive attitude. Believe in yourself, be confident in your abilities and who you are, and a positive attitude will follow.

3. **Surround Yourself With Positive People**
The best way to develop a positive attitude is to surround yourself with other people who have positive attitudes. Take advantage of every opportunity you have to meet new, exciting people, and seek out those who share a positive outlook on life. On the other hand, reconsider relationships you have with people who thrive on negativity and bring you down. Think about what can you do to minimize these relationships' effect on your attitude and to eliminate this kind of negative energy from your life.

4. **Don't Dwell**
Rather than thinking and re-thinking how someone was unkind to you or how you could have done better on a task, think about how you will resolve the situation. Focusing on the positive, proactive things you can do to resolve situations is a better strategy than dwelling on negative feelings.

5. **Be Active**
It's hard to be unhappy when you are busy. Get involved in activities you enjoy, like sports, clubs or volunteering. Having a full life is the foundation of a positive attitude.

6. **Plan Great Things**
Everyone likes to have something to look forward to. Make sure you plan fun weekends, holiday celebrations, and special rewards for yourself.

7. **Learn From Mistakes**
It's not fun to be criticized or realize you have made a mistake. But, rather than focusing on the hurtful and negative aspects of a situation, try to focus on what you can learn from the experience. Remember, true wisdom comes only from making mistakes and then learning from them. Even the most brilliant, respected people in the world have been criticized, rejected and deemed wrong – it's how they became the great people they are!

8. **Be Flexible**
Life is like a roller coaster – you never know when you'll be going up, going down or sent through a loop! To keep a positive attitude, you must be flexible – willing and able to sit back and enjoy life's wild ride.

9. **Communicate Well**
Have you ever paid attention to how you communicate? Do you tend to use more negative statements than positive? How you communicate

Studying - p. 60

When, Where, How Much?

Getting Help

Value of Starting w/ good grades p. 81

p90 Success is more attitude than aptitude

Positive attitude

Get positive in 10 steps

- perspective
- confidence
- positive people
- don't dwell
- be active
- plan
- learn from mistakes
- be flexible
- communicate
- set goals, commit

is a powerful influence on your attitude. Complementing a friend on what a great person they are will make them happy – and make you feel good inside. Likewise, reminding yourself on a regular basis about your strengths, talents and good attributes will help you develop a positive feelings about yourself. It doesn't take much effort to communicate positive thoughts to yourself and others – but it will go a long way toward boosting your positive attitude.

10. Set Goals And Commit To Them
Nothing feels better than reaching a goal you have worked hard to achieve. But you can't reach a goal if you never set one. From something as small as of finishing your homework every night or achieving perfect attendance in a class, to something as big as losing 20 pounds or graduating at the top of your class, goals are an important part of creating a positive attitude. Set short-term and long-term goals, commit to them and enjoy your accomplishments when you reach your goals!

Maintain Your Positive Attitude

So, now you have a positive attitude. Make sure you keep it! To maintain your positive attitude, you must create an environment in which it can thrive. Here's how:

Get Organized
It's hard to be positive when you're surrounded by clutter and disarray. Spend a few minutes each day keeping your living and working areas organized and clean, buy a date book, and create a "to do" list so both your physical environment and thoughts are well-organized.

Be Prepared
Nothing will jump-start a negative attitude faster than being rushed and taken by surprise. Lay out your clothes and pack your bag the night before, review your calendar and "to do" list every morning to make sure you know what to expect for the day. Also, make sure you go everywhere – class, activities, even the grocery store – armed with what you need and prepared for the tasks at hand.

Start Your Day Happy
Why start your day with a blaring alarm? Buy yourself an alarm clock that wakes you with music or a soothing sound. Once you're awake, eat a healthy breakfast – even if you have to pack it the night before and eat it on the run. Make sure you stock your kitchen with healthy, tasty options for breakfast.

Don't Procrastinate
If you always wait until the last minute, you will always be stressed, rushed and behind. Make sure you manage your time well, giving yourself enough

time to prepare for assignments, to travel to and from destinations, and to complete tasks at hand.

Take Care Of Yourself

You can't be positive if you are exhausted, starving and stressing about those extra 15 pounds. Eating well, sleeping enough and exercising regularly are essential to maintaining a long-term positive attitude.

Disconnect

These days, we'd be lost without our TVs, our cell phones, our radios and our computers. Technology is great, but being constantly bombarded by sad headlines, urgent telephone calls, loud radios and spam can take a toll. Take at least a few minutes every day to disconnect yourself from the information overload and reconnect with silence and calm. Just a few minutes spent enjoying the outdoors in silence, reading a novel in a quiet corner of the park, or even meditating can go a long way toward establishing the kind of calm you need to maintain a positive attitude.

Believe it or not, self-esteem can shape your life. Self-esteem is not just a silly concept from some self-help book – it's vital to your success and happiness. Self-esteem begins with you. This chapter will show you how to develop and maintain positive self-esteem by:

- Explaining why self-esteem is important.
- Outlining how self-esteem is developed.
- Recommending strategies for developing strong self-esteem.

What Positive Self-Esteem can do for You

Don't underestimate the power of self-esteem. If you have positive self-esteem, you will:

- ***Believe in yourself and your abilities.***
- ***Focus on your strengths and abilities,*** not your weaknesses and mistakes.
- ***Relish learning new things and meeting challenges.***
- ***Be accountable for your life.***
- ***Overcome adversity.***
- ***Have faith you can achieve your goals.***
- ***Be optimistic.***
- ***Live your life with a sense of purpose.***

The Source of Self-Esteem

Self-esteem isn't a mysterious force that you either have or don't. Self-esteem is developed over time as a result of a variety of forces. Your self-esteem comes from a few key places in your life:

Yourself
The inner voice that tells you who you are is a huge indicator of your self-esteem. Do you believe you are intelligent, talented, kind, skillful? Or do you tell yourself that you are stupid, lazy and unlikeable? Your opinion of yourself is a key source of your self-esteem.

Your Acquaintances
Family, friends, instructors, colleagues, classmates – all of these people play a role in your self-esteem. Are the people who surround you optimistic and life-affirming, or do they complain, criticize, and bring you down? What you hear about yourself from others also helps determine your self-esteem – but it is your responsibility to create an inner circle that accentuates your good qualities, and to tune out the negative chatter – or turn it off altogether.

Your Circumstances – And How You View Them
It may seem that some people have good luck, while other people have no luck at all. But did you know that people actually make their own luck? And, most of the time, luck is all about your perspective. For example, when you do badly on an exam, do you write it off to bad luck, or do you accept your responsibility and view it as an opportunity to do better next time? On the other hand, when you do well on an exam, do you chalk it up to good luck, or do you acknowledge that your success was due to your hard work, talent and knowledge? Your self-esteem is shaped by your circumstances – but even more so by how you view your circumstances and use them to grow as a person.

Tips for Developing Positive Self-Esteem

You are the only one who can develop your self-esteem. If you believe your self-image could use some work, the following strategies can get you on the right track:

- ***Don't compare.*** There's only one you – so why waste your time comparing yourself to others? Instead of focusing on how other people are smarter, more beautiful, more talented or better-liked than you, focus on yourself and what makes you an individual.
- ***Don't dwell.*** Don't waste time dwelling on mistakes or what is wrong with you. Learn from your mistakes and move on, and focus on your strengths and positive attributes.

- ***Be accountable.*** Sometimes it may feel good to blame other people for your mistakes or for what is wrong in your life, but until you can take responsibility for your own role in your circumstances, you won't be able to acknowledge the role you have in the good things in your life either.
- ***Develop diverse skills.*** The more things you learn, and the more opportunities you open yourself up to, the more chances you have to succeed and develop confidence. You won't know if you're good at tennis until you try – so what's stopping you?
- ***Be generous with compliments.*** Recognizing others' for their success and complementing them generously is a great way to emphasize the positive. If you are kind to others, it will help you be kind to yourself as well. And when you receive complements, be gracious – and accept them without excuses.
- ***Take risks.*** Sometimes you have to fail in order to succeed. If you never tackle your fears and try, you'll never know what could have happened. Taking risks and succeeding is a sure-fire way to develop confidence and courage.
- ***Give yourself credit – and rewards.*** Take some time every day to remind yourself of your successes, your talents, and your positive qualities. And be sure to reward yourself when you succeed.
- ***Be grateful.*** Being thankful for what you have is essential to developing a good perspective on your life. When you understand how fortunate you are to have your health, your friends, and your opportunities, then you will be less likely to view every obstacle and every problem as the end of the world. Instead, you will be able to see it in the context of the big picture.
- ***Make yourself a priority.*** Taking care of yourself is important, and the foundation of self-esteem. If you have self-esteem and value yourself, then you will take care of your health.

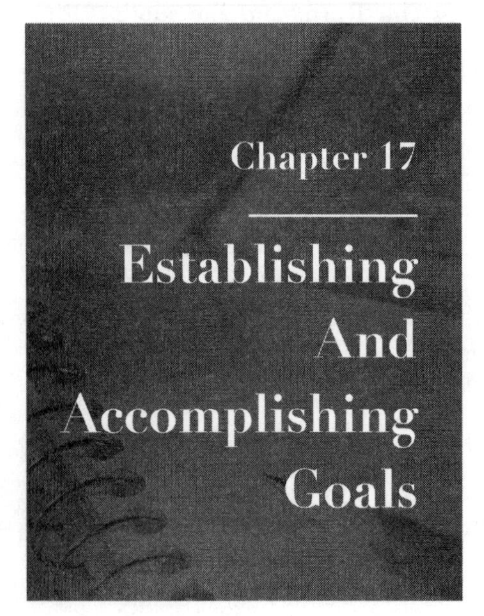

It's a common story: You make a New Year's resolution, and by Valentine's Day you've already forgotten about it. Unfortunately, for every goal that is achieved, there are countless others that aren't. But goals are important.

As a college student, setting goals is how you shape your future. Achieving your goals is how you ensure your success.

Don't let your goals be a casualty of poor planning, low motivation, a bad attitude, or a busy schedule. With a few key strategies, you can set real goals and achieve them.

This chapter will show you how by:

- Giving you a five-step plan for setting goals.
- Recommending strategies to help you set goals you can reach.
- Giving you tips that will help you become and stay motivated.

Five Steps to Establishing Goals

To achieve a goal, you first need to set one. It sounds easy, but to ensure your success, you need to keep in mind a few guidelines while setting goals:

1. **Establish A Goal**
   First, ask yourself what you want to accomplish. Be specific. For example, if you want to improve your grades, be specific about what grades you would like to receive in each of your courses. If you want to get in shape, specify what milestones you would like to achieve. Running a faster mile? Achieving perfect yoga poses? Running a 10K race?

2. **Create An Action Plan**
   How do you accomplish your goal? There is never just one way to accomplish a goal – but if you want to be successful, you must be as specific as possible when you create your plan. If your goal is to run a marathon in eight months, for example, then your action plan should include how many miles you will run each week leading up to the marathon, when you will run each day, what adjustments you will need to make to your diet, and what kind of professional, nutritional or medical advice you will have to seek.
3. **Divide Your Goal Into Smaller Achievements**
   Sometimes reaching a goal can seem like a daunting task. Make it less intimidating by breaking your overall goal into easier, bite-sized goals. For example, if your goal is to lose 20 pounds by summer, create a schedule for how much weight you need to lose each week. Losing one pound a week is less intimidating than focusing only on your 20-pound end goal. And, each week you do lose one pound, your motivation will be renewed and you will be encouraged to achieve your overall goal.
4. **Set A Target Date**
   Setting a goal without developing a timeline is useless. Deciding that you will get out of credit card debt is great, but if you don't set a target date, what does that goal really mean? Does it mean that you will get out of credit card debt before you graduate from college? Before you turn 30? Before you retire?

   Immediately after setting a goal, decide when you will achieve it. Be specific, then develop a timeline that outlines how you will use the time between now and your target date for achieving your goal.
5. **Identify Your Motivators**
   The best way to ensure that you achieve your goal is to determine why you want to achieve it. Do you want to lose weight because you want to look great on the beach this summer? Because you want to improve your health? Because you want to excel at your favorite sport?

   The best way to motivate yourself toward your goal is to focus on why you want to achieve your goal and how great you will feel when you get compliments on your figure at the beach, receive a great doctor's report on your health at your next check-up, or help your team win a championship game.

Establishing Goals that are Realistic

Setting goals that are impossible to achieve is a sure way to frustrate yourself, develop a negative perspective about your goals, and ensure failure. Make sure you develop realistic goals that are designed for success. Here's how:

Prioritize

It's fine to have more than one goal. In fact, most people have multiple goals that focus on various areas of life, including academics, health, relationships and hobbies. However, it's important to remember that to successfully achieve your goals you must prioritize them and focus your attention accordingly. You may want to receive all A's this semester, lose 10 pounds, learn to knit and meet new friends. Which of these goals is most important and urgent to you and your life? Which one can be put on a long-term track? Which one can wait until more time becomes available? The answers won't be the same for everyone, but you know where your priorities lie.

Think Short-Term And Long-Term

Develop your goals like you would build a house. When you build a house, the end result is a comfortable, useful dwelling that fits a family's needs and wants. But to get there various smaller things must be achieved – good design, a strong foundation, expertly installed plumbing and electrical wiring, solid walls and floors, beautiful paint colors and carpets, and comfortable and functional furniture to fill the space. Your goals should work in the same manner.

Your long-term goal may be to achieve a successful career in law. The short-term goals leading up to your career might include excellent grades, a well-rounded resume, great friends and contacts, solid financial plans, and good physical and mental health to support great performance during your career.

Base Goals On Who You Are

Your goals should be a reflection of who you are – your talents, your abilities, your priorities and your deepest desires and needs. When setting goals, try to focus on what you want – not what your parents or your friends want. Your mother may have been the president of her sorority, but you may decide that joining a sorority is not for you. Your father may have enjoyed a long military career, but you may want to achieve a successful career as an educator. Your friends may all be getting jobs after graduation, but you may want to pursue an advanced degree. It may not always be easy, but setting goals that reflect who you are is always the right decision.

Be Specific

Again, setting goals is great. But setting goals that are very specific and have specific timelines and target dates for completion is even better – and more likely to be successful.

Challenge Yourself

The purpose of setting goals is to become a better person. If your goals are too easy to achieve, you won't make any real changes in your life, and you will become easily bored. Challenge yourself! The feeling of achieving a difficult goal is amazing.

Build Reminders Into Your Life
It's easy to lose sight of your goals in the ups and downs of a busy life. Don't let this happen to you. Write down your goals, share them with others and plant constant reminders in visible places. Write goals in your calendar, keep a goals "to do" list, tape a list of goals to your refrigerator, or even create a screen saver on your computer that lists your goals as a visual reminder.

Be Flexible
Getting sidetracked happens to the best of us. Life changes, and so should our goals. Instead of getting frustrated and giving up when your plans get off track, be flexible and create new solutions for achieving your goals – even if it means that you need to take more time, revise your goals, or seek help.

Becoming – and Staying – Motivated

Your motivation level is probably the most important factor in determining your success. Getting and staying highly motivated is the best way to guarantee that you will reach your goal. Easier said than done, but motivation isn't a completely elusive quality. Implement these strategies to make sure you develop the motivation you need:

Focus On Results
Focusing on the positive things that will happen when you achieve your goal is a great way to keep yourself motivated. Say your goal is to achieve an "A" in chemistry. Throughout the term, without a doubt you will have moments where it is difficult to get out of bed to attend chemistry lecture, when you would rather spend time with friends than study for chemistry, where skipping a meeting with your instructor to leave early for a weekend trip to the beach seems really appealing.

When you begin to waver on your plans to achieve your goal, spend a few minutes thinking about how great it will feel to see an "A" next to "chemistry" on your report card, how proud your parents will be, how this high grade in chemistry and the knowledge you gained during the class will help you achieve your overall goal of earning admission to a top medical school. Focusing on positive end results will make the difficult moments easier to overcome.

Share
A great strategy for achieving your goals is to share your goals with friends and family. Ask your friends to monitor your achievements and check in on your progress from time to time. Knowing that others are aware of your

goals will help keep you on track, and the interest and encouragement of people close to you will help to keep you focused and enthusiastic about your goals.

Reward Yourself

It's important to take time to celebrate your achievements, even the small ones. As you progress toward your goal, pat yourself on the back every step of the way. Build time into your schedule to allow yourself to do something fun, budget money to buy small rewards like dinner from your favorite restaurant or a movie, and give yourself permission to congratulate yourself on a job well done.

Everyone complains that they need more time in the day. As a busy college student, you could probably list a hundred things you would do with an extra hour or an extra day. But did you know that you could actually give yourself more time?

No, it's not some secret that magically adds a 25th hour to the day or an eighth day to the week. It's called good time management – and it's really fairly simple to do.

This chapter will show you how by:

- Showing you how to assess your use of time.
- Recommending strategies to take control of your time and manage it well.
- Outlining time zappers that students are prone to – and how to avoid them.

How do You use Your Time?

To manage your time well, you need to get a clear picture of how you currently use your time so you can assess how you can use it better. Spend one week tracking how you use your time – from how long you spend in the shower each day to how many hours you watch television to how many hours you spend sleeping, eating, studying, attending class and talking on the phone. You should actually make a chart of each hour of the day, next to which you list what you did during that time.

You will probably be very surprised to find out just how much time you spend doing things you don't feel are important (*watching junk television, paging through catalogs, or surfing the net, for example*) and how few hours you spend on the things that are your top priorities – like studying, working out, enjoying your hobbies and spending time with friends and family.

After you have charted how you spend your time and can see how your time was spent over the course of a week, assess how you would like to use your time differently. Do you want more time to work out? To read? To visit your mother? Do you wish you could shave a few hours off of your television viewing or net surfing, or reduce the time you spend running errands? List the changes you want to make, then work on an action plan to make the changes a reality.

Manage Your Time Well

Taking control of your time requires you to develop a plan of action. To do this you will need a calendar of your entire school term and what must be accomplished when, and a weekly plan of how you will spend your time to accomplish what you need to. Here's how:

Create A Term Calendar

This calendar serves as a quick reference to all the major events that will take place during this term. Don't forget anything: school assignments, club meetings, family events like weddings or parties, doctor's appointments, personal projects, vacations and holidays, visits from friends or family, etc. Use a large calendar that is easy to read and fits where you want it – on your desk, wall, even on your computer screen. Remember:

- ***Use the right calendar.*** A free online calendar sounds neat – but won't be useful if you don't want to take the time to turn on your computer and visit the Web site every time you need to refer to it. Likewise, that free calendar from your mechanic may be free, but if there's not enough room to write in all your commitments, or it rips every time you turn the page, it's not useful.
- ***Use your syllabi*** to write in all important due dates, deadlines and exams.
- ***Review your term calendar regularly*** – at least once a week, if not more.
- ***Resolve conflicts immediately*** – even if they are weeks or months away. The earlier you resolve conflicts, the fewer problems will result.

Create A Weekly Plan

As the term begins, map out a rough plan for each week of the term that allows you enough time to achieve what you need to achieve. Then, before the start of each week, sit down and write a detailed plan of the week ahead, including a to-do list and an hour-by-hour breakdown of each day. Remember:

- ***Schedule time each week to create your weekly plan for the next week!***
- ***Write in all activities you must attend,*** like class, meetings and appointments.
- ***Review your term calendar*** as you are creating your weekly plan to make sure you don't overlook any deadlines, commitments or engagements.
- ***Give yourself some flexibility*** to accommodate unseen circumstances or events. For example, you may plan to grocery shop at noon on Wednesday, but then find that a traffic accident would cause your shopping trip to last far too long to make it worth it. If you have no room in your weekly schedule for an unforeseeable event like this, you will have to forgo shopping – and end up starving or going without toothpaste as a result!
- ***Resolve conflicts immediately.*** Don't wait until the day before you have both a meeting scheduled and the need to study for a test the next morning. Decide if you can study at another time, or let your club know well in advance that you won't be able to attend the meeting that week.

Common Time Zappers

Procrastination

We're all guilty of it at one time or another. Whether we organize our junk drawer when we should be writing a paper or trick ourselves into thinking we have plenty of time to watch television when we really have a project due in less than 24 hours, we have all fooled ourselves into thinking we are doing other important things that need to be accomplished instead of getting to the real task at hand. Procrastination is the biggest time sapper known to mankind. Avoid procrastinating by:

- ***Creating a realistic schedule*** for completing tasks that leave extra time for unforseeable circumstances.
- ***Keeping a positive, motivated attitude.***
- ***Breaking tasks and projects into manageable blocks,*** with breaks built in.
- ***Rewarding yourself for a job well done*** – and giving yourself something to look forward to.
- ***Getting support.*** Find a friend who has to complete the same task you do and work together. Take a time management class or ask your advisor for tips on how to eliminate procrastination.
- ***Avoiding negativity.*** The more you complain or think about how you really don't want to complete a task, the more stress you create and the more time you put between you and the accomplishment of your goal.

Interruptions

If you're constantly interrupted, you can't possibly manage your time and stick to a schedule. The world is full of potential interruptions – the trick is to manage them. Here's how:

- ***Learn to say no.*** If you are in the middle of completing an important task and someone stops by to ask you to join them in an activity or help them with their own task, you need to learn how to say no. You don't have to be rude – just let them know that you are busy, but would be happy to help or come by at another time. Ask them to call you or stop by again to set up a time.
- ***Ask that your time be respected.*** Establish a study time or set times to complete tasks, then let your roommates, friends and family know about your schedule and ask them not to call you, stop by, or expect to hear from/see you during these times. If putting a friendly or humorous sign on your door or message on your answering machine helps, then do it.
- ***Turn off phone ringers, televisions, computers, etc.*** Some of the biggest interruptions are the ring of your cell phone or home phone, the beep of your incoming e-mail box and the temptation of that television show you can't resist. Avoid the urge to answer the phone or look at e-mail by turning everything off before you begin your task.
- ***Get organized.*** Getting down to business and finding out that you have to go out to buy printer paper to print out your notes or paper towels to clean up the coffee from last night that you just spilled on your notebook is anything but good time management. If you are organized, you will save time and frustration.

Your Internal Clock

If you have the urge to fall asleep at 2 p.m. every day, it's probably not efficient or effective to plan to study at that time. If you know you can't keep your eyes open past 11 p.m., don't schedule time to finally organize your desk at that time – you'll never do it. Believe it or not, your own internal clock can be a huge time sapper if you try to work against it instead of with it.

Information Overload

Cell phones, PDAs, e-mail, answering machines, Internet news sites, online blogs and magazines jamming your mailbox to the point of overflow. With everything we have to keep up with these days, we could spend all day just listening to messages, answering e-mails, entering information into our PDA and reading the Web sites, publications and blogs that have somehow become necessary. Don't fall into the trap of information overload – you don't have to do and know it all. Don't feel pressured to stay up-to-date with your favorite television show just because all your friends are. Don't feel compelled to answer every silly joke forwarded by e-mail with a thank you or a personal note. So what if you miss today's headlines? Tomorrow they will just be yesterday's news, and you probably have better things to do with your time.

Chapter 19

Listening

Ask yourself this: have you ever been involved in a conversation and realized that you haven't heard what was being said to you? Have you ever left a lecture or speech and discovered that you couldn't adequately explain the important points that the speaker was trying to emphasize? Chances are, the answer to both of these questions is yes. All of us, at one time or another, are guilty of being poor listeners.

On the other hand, can you recall a conversation you had with someone during which you felt like you really understood that person, and that person was truly engaged in what you were saying? Do you have a friend or relative to whom you always turn to discuss important things in your life because you know they will understand? Then you understand what it's like to truly be listened to.

Being an effective listener is important to your overall achievement, your academic, professional and personal relationships, and your ability to communicate well with the people who are important to you and your success. Being a good listener is about more than just hearing – it's about committing yourself to being engaged with the people and world around you.

Developing good listening skills is essential to your success – both as a college student and in the future. This chapter will show you how to become a better listener by:

- Explaining the difference between merely hearing and truly listening.
- Outlining the benefits of active listening.
- Recommending strategies for developing strong listening skills.

The Difference between Hearing and Listening

Hearing and listening are two very different actions. Hearing, quite simply, means that you are aware of sound. Listening is the purposeful action of engaging with that sound and trying to absorb, understand and be influenced by what you are hearing.

Hearing someone is easy. Listening to them is more difficult, but much more powerful, and useful. When you are truly listening you:

- ***Show your interest and support***, and put the speaker at ease.
- ***Take the time to clear up misconceptions and check assumptions.***
- ***Restate what has been said to you*** to demonstrate your understanding and aid retention of what you have heard.
- ***Ask respectful clarifying questions.***
- ***Search for the key points and issues.***
- ***Encourage the speaker to talk*** by providing him/her the time to say what needs to be said, and by minimizing distractions and interruptions.

Why Listening is Important

Do you remember the childhood game of telephone? In this game, someone whispers a statement in the ear of another player and the statement is then repeated in whispers down a long line of people. At the end, the final statement is said aloud and compared to the original statement. Usually the resulting statement is a hilariously distorted and barely recognizable form of what was originally said. Funny, yes – but it is also a great example of how communication can fail when people don't listen well. Don't let your communications end up like a bad game of telephone – you'll miss out on too much. When you listen well, you:

- ***Learn and understand.*** If you become an active listener, you will be amazed at how much more you learn and understand.
- ***Increase efficiency.*** When you don't have to ask people to repeat themselves, when your understanding is clear and deep, and when you can take better notes, you will improve your efficiency greatly.
- ***Improve relationships.*** A primary reason that relationships falter is because people do not understand each other. Actively listening to the individuals who are important to you personally, academically and professionally will help you to better understand them and their needs – improving your relationships.
- ***Create opportunities.*** Listening actively helps you remember names, read between the lines, and develop stronger relationships – all important

components of discovering and developing opportunities for yourself in your academic career and beyond.

- ***Speak better.*** To be a great speaker, you need to listen to what is being asked of you and be able to respond. When you listen actively, you will do a better job of understanding what you need to speak about, and how you need to say it to communicate well.

Become a Good Listener

Are you a good listener? How can you tell? And what makes a good listener, anyway? There is no one right answer, but the following strategies are the foundation for every good listener's skills:

Find Your Motivation
To listen well, you have to want to listen. In other words, you need to be motivated to focus on what is being said. To do this, think about why it is important for you to listen. For example, listening well during lectures will help you achieve better grades. Listening well during an interview could help you land the internship of your dreams. Listening well to your parents will help you better understand them and deepen your relationship. Focusing on the reason listening is important will help you maintain your concentration as you listen.

Concentrate
Concentration is key to successful listening. But concentrating is easier said than done, right? It's not always an easy task to stay focused on a conversation when you're in a loud restaurant, on a lecture when you're in a crowded lecture hall, or on a job interview when you're nervous and distracted by a phone ringing in the reception area. You can set yourself up to concentrate better with a few strategies. Here's how:

- ***Familiarize yourself.*** Whenever possible, make sure you are familiar with the information being discussed. Before lectures, complete assignments and reading, and review notes. To prepare for interviews or meetings, do your research and know about the company, your qualifications, etc. It's always easier to maintain your focus when you're one step ahead of the game.

- ***Be prepared.*** Arrive early, have the materials you need, and physically and mentally prepare yourself to concentrate on what is being said.

- ***Create the right environment.*** It's not always possible to completely control your environment, but do what you can to minimize distractions and annoyances. Don't sit next to noisy or distracting people. Choose a seat far away from doors and windows. Avoid chairs placed on squeaky floorboards or tables with uneven legs.

- ***Position yourself.*** There's a reason that front-row concert tickets come at a premium. It's easier to concentrate when you can actually hear and see what's going on. To maximize your listening potential, position yourself as close as possible to the speaker so you can pick up on body language, expressions and voice inflections that can influence meaning.
- ***Make eye contact.*** Making eye contact with a speaker, even if that speaker is an instructor speaking to 100 students in a lecture hall, will make it feel like he/she is speaking directly to you and help you maintain your focus.

Be Objective

If you go into a conversation or lecture with pre-formed opinions and thoughts about what is going to be said or who is going to be saying it, it will only hinder your ability to truly listen. To really listen, you must tune out the inner voice that makes judgments, focus on what is being said, and nothing more.

Get Involved

Believe it or not, listening really is an interactive activity. While you must maintain a reasonable amount of silence to give the speaker ample time and opportunity to make their point, you also must get involved in the communication process. Try asking clarifying and probing questions, summarizing the facts and feelings of what is being said, reframing the important points and issues, and restating what is being said for clarification.

Practice

Listening, like all skills, can improve with practice. During college you will have many opportunities to practice the listening skills that will serve you well for a lifetime. Make sure you regularly use these strategies during lectures and important conversations, and gauge how well you are listening by comparing your lecture notes with other students to see what you missed. You even can ask people if you effectively captured what they were saying.

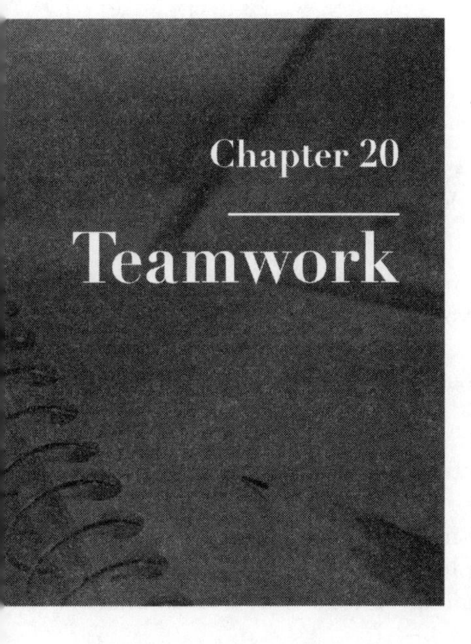

Chapter 20

Teamwork

According to the Webster's Dictionary, teamwork is defined as:

Work done by a number of associates, usually each doing a clearly defined portion, but all subordinating personal prominence to the efficiency of the whole.

Sounds fairly simple, but everyone knows that teamwork can be anything but. If you're like most people, you can probably recall times in your life when working on a team had disastrous results (*remember that 11th grade prom planning committee?*), as well as a time when working on a team was difficult but resulted in rewarding and amazing results (*have you ever been part of a winning sports team?*). At its worst, teamwork can produce anger, frustration, resentment – and bring a project to a complete standstill. At its best, teamwork can inspire creativity, innovation, productivity and amazing results.

Whatever your feelings about working on a team, don't dismiss teamwork as something that isn't relevant or important to you. In recent years the list of skills named by employers as essential has expanded to include teamwork – right near the top.

Chances are, you already have experience working on a team and know what kind of "team player" you are. Maybe you already know you need to develop better teamwork skills. Perhaps you already are a great team player – but even that's not enough. To be a true teamwork pro who is a real asset to employers, you need to know how to do more than just work well with others. A teamwork pro knows how to motivate others to be good team players, create a winning team, get the most out the team you have, and conquer the most common obstacles facing teams.

This chapter will show you how by:

- Explaining what makes a good team player.
- Describing the qualities of a successful team.
- Recommending strategies for getting the most out of a team.

What is a Team Player?

Remember picking teams for grade school kickball? There were a few kids everyone wanted on their team. And there were the kids who always got picked last – you know who they were. Aside from their kickball skills and talents, what were the qualities that the first-picked kids possessed? Were they easy to work with? Fun? Encouraging?

The real world isn't all that different from your kickball days – some people are the kinds of people you want on your team; others are the kind you avoid at all costs. To be the kind of individual what is a welcome addition to any team, you must be:

- ***Skillful.*** Everyone wants someone on their team who has talents and skills. And every team needs a group of people with diverse skills. Are you a good writer, a good speaker, a math whiz, great with Internet research? All of these are skills that could make you a valuable member of a team. Develop your skills, play them up – and let others know what you are good at.
- ***Cooperative.*** A good team player pulls their weight, minimizes conflict, stays positive, and brings out the best in teammates.
- ***A good communicator.*** Failure to communicate well is one of the biggest sources of conflict – and failure – in teams. Effective communication is one of the most important facets of a successful team.
- ***Committed.*** A good team player lets their teammates know they are committed to the common cause and that they can be counted on to keep their commitments.
- ***Honest.*** Honesty is vital to identifying and discussing problems, establishing trust between team members, and creating an open working environment. A good team player doesn't withhold information, gossip or back stab.
- ***Willing to share the credit,*** not the blame. A good team player takes responsibility for their actions – even their mistakes. What's more, a good team player knows how to give credit where credit is due.

Successful Teams

So you have a team made up of great team players – a good first step. Now what? To create success, teams as a whole must possess:

- ***Purpose.*** The team must understand what the problem is and the importance of arriving at a solution.
- ***Empowerment.*** A strong team feels empowered to work and create solutions – with the support of their leaders and the resources they need to succeed.
- ***Strong relationships.*** A good team has members who work well together.
- ***Good communication.*** A good team has members who know how to listen, speak and discusss.
- ***Flexibility.*** A good team can adapt and adjust to changing circumstances and expectations.
- ***Productivity.*** A good team works smart and gets the job done.
- ***Morale.*** A good team has high morale and can keep morale high even amid pressure and difficult circumstances.

Get the Most Out of Working with a Team

To be a true teamwork pro, you need to understand how to make a team situation work – despite the obstacles, difficulties and problems. By implementing a few strategies, you can ensure teamwork success. To get the most out of a team:

- ***Create clear goals.*** Team members must understand what their goals are, believe the goals are important, know what they are expected to accomplish, and understand how they will work together to achieve those goals.
- ***Go for small victories.*** To build an effective team, you should focus on small, short-term successes to build the confidence that is necessary to achieve the overall, big-picture goal.
- ***Build mutual trust.*** Trust is a fragile thing in a group; it takes a long time to build up and can be destroyed very quickly. To build trust, team members must be approachable, respectful, objective, dependable and willing to listen to each other's ideas.
- ***Ensure mutual accountability and a sense of common purpose.*** For a team to be a real team, all members must feel accountable – for both successes and failures.

- ***Secure the resources you need.*** If team success is dependent on resources from outside sources, it is important to make sure those resources are there.
- ***Develop the skills you need.*** Team members – and the team itself – may need some training to build skills. The training may need to be in problem solving, communication, negotiation, conflict-resolution – or even in something as simple as facts and information about the topic at hand, math or accounting skills, or writing.
- ***Be willing to change the team's membership.*** No matter how difficult it may be, at times it may be necessary to change the make-up of a team.

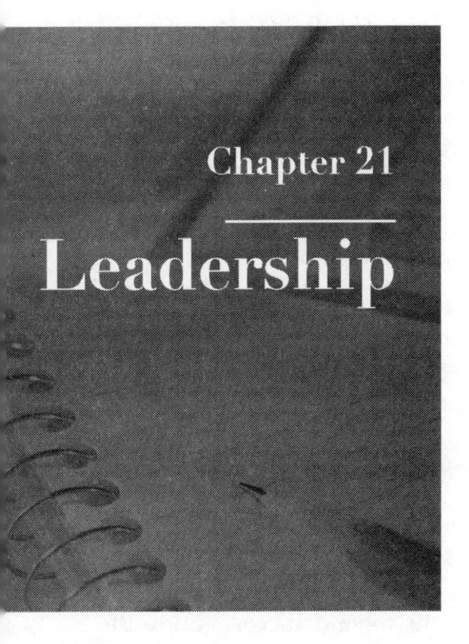

Everyone aspires to be a leader. Leaders are successful. Leaders inspire people. Leaders change the world. But what is a leader, exactly? And how do you become one?

A leader takes people where they want to go. A great leader takes people where they don't necessarily want to go but ought to be.

— *Rosalynn Carter*

Leaders aren't born, they are made. And they are made just like anything else, through hard work. And that's the price we'll have to pay to achieve that goal, or any goal.

— *Vince Lombardi*

Leadership is doing what is right when no one is watching.

— *George Van Valkenburg*

It's a challenge to define leadership. It's an even bigger challenge to become a leader. But there are some common characteristics that all leaders share, and some real ways to develop the skills you need to be a leader. Your college years are a great time to develop leadership skills, practice your skills by accepting leadership roles, and define yourself as the kind of leader you want to be.

This chapter will show you how by:

- Explaining why leadership is important.
- Defining what a leader is.
- Recommending strategies for developing the skills you need to be a successful leader.

Why Leadership Matters

In today's quickly changing world, we can no longer take for granted that our past goals are still relevant or viable, or that the way we used to do things will always be efficient and effective. In order to succeed and progress in this day and age, we must continually set new goals, envision new solutions, invent new ways of doing things, and adapt to the dynamic and challenging environments in which we live. To do this we need great leaders to show us the way.

Many people believe that the ability to adapt is the key to success. But talent and ability are only the first steps to success. To finish the journey we need leadership. Leadership makes the difference between good companies and great ones, between adequate governments and those that make lives better, between education that teaches facts and skills and education that inspires people to truly learn and be their best. Remember:

- ***Leadership can have a beneficial and powerful impact*** on virtually every part of your life.
- ***You need more than technical skills to be successful in business.*** In fact, the most talented and skilled individuals are not always the leaders. Those who set goals, inspire action, and creatively change as needed will always manage even more talented individuals who lack leadership skills.
- ***Without proper leadership people stop working,*** nobody listens, teamwork fails, some employees and customers leave, and people pick on each other.

Not everyone will be a great leader, but everyone can – and must – display leadership. Whether you want to be a successful business owner, executive, sales manager, doctor, lawyer, teacher, artist, politician or social activist, the qualities of leadership will be important to you, to your success and to the people who depend on you. Using your college years to develop the skills and qualities you need to be a leader is one of the most important things you will do at this time in your life.

The Qualities of a Leader

There are all different kinds of leaders. Coaches, teachers, CEOs, religious figures, political activists, medical and scientific groundbreakers, event organizers, soldiers – even unlikely heroes that lead in times of trouble at the spur of the moment. Every leader accomplishes different goals and employs different strategies and tactics to establish their leadership. However, there are several qualities that are vital to a leader's success. A leader:

- ***Has vision.*** It's simple: To be able to lead, you must be able to clearly see and define where you want to go. A good leader can state what the future will look like and explain, in no uncertain terms, how they will get there.
- ***Motivates people.*** Leaders understand that you can't get anywhere alone. That's why great leaders understand what motivates people

– and that it's not always what you may assume. For example, many people are surprised to find that a large salary is not a great motivator. Great leaders understand that praise, appreciation and recognition are stronger motivators than money alone.

- ***Is emotionally intelligent.*** Emotional intelligence is a catchphrase that has been batted around a lot in recent years. Very simply, someone who is emotionally intelligent has the ability to identify, use, understand and manage emotions – both other people's and their own. Being able to read people, empathize with their feelings and use your understanding to effectively lead them is invaluable to every leader.
- ***Empowers people.*** A good leader understands that they can't do everything – and that they will be more powerful and successful by trusting people, letting them know what is expected from them, and giving them the tools and the power to do what needs to be done. Working toward a goal by yourself may help you to make progress; empowering ten others to work with you practically guarantees success.
- ***Is trustworthy and has integrity.*** No one will follow a leader who is distrustful, unfair or inconsistent in their values and beliefs. An honest leader who lives life without contradiction will be respected and effective – even when people don't agree with their viewpoint.
- ***Takes risks.*** If you always do things the way they always have been done, you'll only get more of the same results. In order to truly effect change or make progress, you have to break away from what is safe and take risks. Leaders understand this and have learned how to take smart risks that payoff big.
- ***Focuses and follows through.*** A real leader understands how to focus on the task at hand, set priorities for success, and finish what has been started.
- ***Has a sense of humor.*** This is perhaps one of the most important leadership qualities. A leader must have a sense of humor, use it to laugh at themselves when necessary, put things in perspective, and defuse difficult situations with laughter.

You now know the major qualities of a leader. But what else do good leaders do? Good leaders also:

- ***Make others feel good about themselves,*** as well as the work they are doing.
- ***Energize others.***
- ***Keep an open mind*** and accept that good ideas can come from anyone and everyone.
- ***Communicate well.***

- ***Delegate effectively*** by assigning responsibilities wisely.
- ***Avoid wasting time*** by not playing political games.
- ***Embrace responsibility and are accountable.***
- ***Set a good example*** by displaying a high level of professionalism and dedication.
- ***Listen well*** in order to know what is going on around them. Listening opens doors to genuine communication and also demonstrates respect and caring for others.
- ***Encourage feedback*** and have an open-door policy so people know they are willing to listen and provide solutions.
- ***Offer recognition*** by publicly giving praise for efforts and achievements.
- ***Create an environment*** that promotes constant learning.
- ***Never abuse the power they hold.***
- ***Define success in their own terms*** and never let others make rules for their own happiness.

Be a Leader

While it's true that some people are born with the characteristics that make them natural leaders, you don't have to inherit leadership – you can develop it. Even if you aren't a "natural born leader," you can become a leader with a little work. Conversely, even those who are born leaders sometimes neglect their natural talents, exploit them for the wrong causes, or refuse to develop them – or use them altogether. The old adage really is true: Great leaders aren't born – they're made.

So what kinds of things can you do during your college years to develop the skills you need to lead? To become a leader you need to:

- ***Know yourself.*** It may sound easy, but getting to know yourself – your talents, strengths and skills, as well as your flaws and weaknesses – is the foundation of your leadership development. Take an honest inventory of your qualities and how they relate to your strengths as a leader. Which of the leadership qualities discussed earlier do you possess? Which do you need to work on? What talents and skills do you have that will make your role as a leader easier? Which of your character flaws will make it more difficult? Take a well-known and respected personality test if you need some help. Assess your personality qualities, take stock of your strengths and weaknesses, and make a plan for improvement.
- ***Develop a leadership philosophy.*** Not every leader has the same values, perspectives, or way of leading. There is no "right" way to lead, but leaders must have a clear leadership philosophy. What is yours going

to be? Pay attention to the kinds of leaders you admire, think about the leaders who have made a difference in your life, do a little research into different kinds of leadership, and take a hard look at your own beliefs about what works when it comes to leadership. Think of your leadership philosophy as a mission statement for how you will live your life as a leader.

- ***Be the best at what you do.*** Developing leadership skills is essential. But, if you are a hack in your field, it is unlikely that anyone will consider you a leader, no matter how strong your leadership skills are. If you want to be a leader in the field of computer technology, learn how to be a great computer programmer first. Aspiring to be a leader and visionary in the film industry? Learn how to be an expert actor, director or screenwriter. A great politician? Get a great education and background in political science.
- ***Surround yourself with good people*** – including mentors. If you fill your life with positive, creative and diverse people, you can't help but develop leadership skills! Seek out people who possess leadership qualities and find a broad range of mentors from whom you can learn.
- ***Watch leaders you admire.*** Surely you admire a broad range of leaders – from teachers you have had to the political leaders who make headlines. Pay attention to these leaders and what they do – and try to define exactly what it is about them that you admire. Why are they effective leaders? What do they do that commands attention and respect? Why are people compelled to follow them? You can learn a lot about leadership and how you can cultivate it by watching the leaders who make a difference to you.
- ***Practice by doing.*** Great leaders become who they are by starting young and taking small, progressive steps toward their goals. U.S. senators were high school class presidents and college club leaders first; CEOs most likely started young as Eagle Scouts and debate club presidents. As a college student, you are surrounded by opportunities to be a leader – it's up to you to step up to the plate and assume the role. Something as small as being your dorm floor representative or campus environmental club committee head can be ideal for helping you practice the skills you need to be a great leader.
- ***Develop communication skills.*** Strong communications skills are perhaps the most important factor in your success as a leader. To effectively lead, you must be able to listen actively, define your vision with words, speak clearly, and write well. Think about communication in the same way you think about math or science: a discipline you must study and master in order to succeed. Use every available opportunity to develop your listening, writing and speaking skills, then practice these skills whenever you can.

If you're like a lot of college students, you probably think that networking is not relevant to you. For many college students, the word "networking" conjures images of professionals and business owners exchanging cards, creating Rolodexes and mouthing the words "call me" or "we'll do lunch." This is a hopelessly dated understanding of networking. Networking is really just the process of developing personal and professional relationships with the purpose of exchanging information, advice, contacts and support. And networking is not simply relevant to college students – it's vital.

Have you ever heard the saying, "It's not what you know, it's who you know?" Well, often this is absolutely true. In the real world, people often land jobs, earn promotions, receive recognition, get help, perks and freebies, garner invites and discover opportunities as a result of the power of networking. Done well, networking can create a diverse support network that can be an invaluable resource to help you achieve success.

This chapter will show you how to network effectively by:

- Explaining where and when to find networking opportunities.
- Recommending strategies designed to help you create an invaluable network of support.
- Giving you tips on how to best use your network once you have created it.

Find Opportunities

Networking opportunities are plentiful if you know where to look. Sometimes the opportunities are obvious, while other times you may find the chance to build your network in the most unlikely places. Here are a few common opportunities to keep in mind:

College Activities
Clubs, sports, trips, social events, associations, student government – all of these activities are great ways to meet the kinds of people who could be perfect for your network. Don't count anyone out – fellow college students, graduate students, instructors or alumni advisors, even panelists, speakers or guests who are invited to appear at a meeting or event. Going a little outside of your core interests might be a good idea, too – go on a college-sponsored ski trip, for example, even if you're a novice skier, to expose yourself to a diverse group of people.

Family
Out of a desire to be independent, you may be tempted to turn down your father's offer to introduce you to his old college roommate who is now an executive at the company where you really want an internship. Don't. Viewing your family as part of your network is actually a great strategy. Your parents, your siblings, grandparents, aunts and uncles, cousins – all of them have a huge interest in helping you (*they love you, after all!*), and all probably have an extensive network of their own. Make sure your immediate and extended family knows about your ambitions so they can keep their eyes open for opportunities, to help you out.

Friends
When you are a college student, your friends become your family away from home. You'd probably do anything for your closest friends – and they'd probably do anything for you. Don't overlook your friends as ways to develop your network. Perhaps your roommate's father is in the same line of work that you are considering. Maybe one of your friends is the niece of the CEO of an organization where you want a summer internship. Or you could have a friend who is an expert at networking and could give you some tips, introduce you to some key people, or take you along to meetings or social gatherings where networking is the goal.

Instructors
One reason your instructors have chosen a career in college teaching is that they want to help prepare young people for their futures and give them every opportunity to succeed – which includes serving as a mentor and contact for their students. Developing relationships with your instructors that extend outside of the classroom is a great way to network.

Advisors
Your advisors can provide you with a wealth of knowledge. If you need help deciding which activities to pursue, leads on internships, suggestions on how to go about an internship search, or career recommendations, chances are your advisor will have some great advice. Your advisor is likely to be well connected in your college community, and in the local community as well.

Career Fairs
Throughout the year you will find that a variety of career fairs take place on your campus or in the local community. Sometimes these fairs are sponsored by your college and held in a campus auditorium, other times you may see a career fair advertised that is sponsored by a local company or organization seeking to broaden their work force. Even if you are not close to graduation, these career fairs can be worthwhile. Put on a suit, polish your resume and attend – just to meet key people, ask for advice, and get your name and face out there.

Professional Associations
To further their career, professionals often are active members of associations designed to meet the needs of people who work in their specific field. For example, there are a variety of medical associations for doctors, bar associations for lawyers, restaurant associations for restaurant owners and workers, public relations societies for public relations professionals, even art leagues for professional artists. Throughout the year these kinds of associations will hold a variety of events – many of which are open, for a fee, to non-members. Some associations even welcome "student" members for a reduced-cost membership fee. Do a little research to find out if there is an association for the career you are considering, then look into attending an event or joining as a student. It's a great way to meet people in your chosen field.

Develop Your Network

So, you've met a lot of great new people and have lots of networking opportunities on the horizon. Now what? Once you've made the contacts, it's up to you to develop effective relationships that are mutually supportive. For any networking relationship to work, it must be a win-win situation, where both people benefit.

Sometimes it's easy to figure out how a relationship can be mutually beneficial. For example, friends enjoy each other's company, make each other laugh, help each other through bad times and offer support and love. But what about an instructor who may be able to write you a recommendation letter? Or the CEO of a successful local company who you met at an alumni dinner, who might be able to offer you a job when you graduate? It's easy to see what these individuals can offer you, but what can you offer them? It may surprise you, but you actually have a lot to offer. You can offer them:

- ***Attention*** – Everyone loves to be the center of attention and feel that people are interested in them. Asking lots of questions and showing enthusiasm for someone's career, interests and life can be a great way to develop a relationship.
- ***Passion*** – People recognize and are attracted to passion. When you are passionate about your interests, your future career, your academics, your hobbies and life in general, you are someone who people want to get to know.
- ***Gratitude*** – For most people, nothing feels better than hearing "thank you." When someone offers you help, support or opportunities, do whatever you can to show your appreciation.

Use Your Network

You can develop the most comprehensive and diverse network known to mankind, but if you are too shy or afraid to use the contacts you've developed, your network won't do you an ounce of good. When you need help, ask for it!

If you are searching for an internship, ask appropriate contacts if they know of any opportunities and give them your resume. If you need a part-time job, ask relevant contacts if any are available at their company. When it comes time for graduation, make sure all of your contacts know what kind of job you are looking for, are aware that you may be using them as references, and have copies of your resume to pass on should they find an opportunity that is right for you.

On the flip side, remember that networking is a two-way street, and it also will be asked for help from time to time. Make sure you help out should one of your corporate contacts ask you to organize a college team for their company's charity race, or if someone wants to use you as a reference, for example.

Stress. Late nights. Greasy cheeseburgers at the cafeteria. The Freshman fifteen. If you think these things go hand in hand with the college experience, you're right.

Many college students endure high levels of stress, sleepless nights, annoying illnesses, poor diets, non-existent exercise plans and the unwelcome addition of more than a few extra pounds. But it doesn't have to be that way. In fact, smart college students understand that maintaining good health is essential to a successful – and enjoyable – college career.

College is challenging enough – if you're feeling physically ill, emotionally drained, exhausted, and guilty about bad habits, you're just adding unnecessarily to the challenge. Making your health a priority isn't just a good idea – it's essential to your success.

This chapter will show you how to improve, guard and maintain your good health by:

- Outlining the essential areas of well-being: diet, exercise, sleep, stress management, illness prevention, and dealing with depression.
- Recommending strategies for a healthy lifestyle.
- Explaining the most common health risks and how to manage them.

Diet

You know that a good diet is an important building block of good health. You learned about the food pyramid in grade school. Years of health classes and daily reminders from your mother to eat your vegetables drove the point home. But now that you're a busy college student, maintaining good eating habits has become difficult. Good food choices must now compete with convenience, a tight schedule, and temptation at every turn in the form of fast-food joints, late-night pizza delivery and college cafeterias that cater to students' demand for greasy food.

It's no wonder that many new college students gain the proverbial Freshman Fifteen. The good news is that recent studies indicate that the Freshman Fifteen is somewhat of a myth – most new college students do not gain fifteen pounds. The bad news is that the same studies reveal that the majority of college freshman do gain weight in their first year– about six pounds for men and four-and-a-half pounds for women. You don't have to become a statistic. Raising your awareness, understanding risk factors, and implementing a few key strategies can help you maintain good eating habits in the face of the challenges you face in the college environment.

Understanding College Weight Gain

Weight gain is very individual. Every person gains weight in different ways and for different reasons. But there are several common denominators in college students who gain weight. Students who gain weight:

- ***Aren't skilled*** in creating a balanced diet.
- ***Lack discipline*** and eat what they want, when they want it.
- ***Eat irregularly***, skipping meals and snacking late at night.
- ***Maintain a diet laden with high-fat, high-calorie and nutritionally empty foods*** like fast food and alcoholic beverages.
- ***Turn to unhealthy convenience foods*** when they are short on time.
- ***Often eat to deal with stress*** or emotional turmoil.
- ***Don't sleep enough.***
- ***Skip exercise*** and/or lack healthy physical activity.

Evading College Weight Gain

Unhealthy college weight gain is not inevitable. With a little work, even the busiest college students can maintain a healthy eating plan. A healthy eating plan is:

- ***Realistic*** and designed to fit your life.
- ***Not based on fad diets.***
- ***Focused on moderation and nutritional quality***, not deprivation and calorie counting.

To develop an eating plan that works for you:

- ***Check into the health resources offered through your college*** and make an appointment with your college physician or other health experts who might be available to you through your student health center or gym, like nutritionists or dieticians.
- ***Visit school health centers and gyms*** that may offer seminars and classes on healthy eating.
- ***Research nutrition and healthy eating*** on the Internet or at your school library.

A Word On Weight Loss

It's natural to be worried about weight gain during your college years, but some college students focus too much on their weight. For some vulnerable college students, what begins as a diet and fitness plan turns into an eating disorder like anorexia, bulimia or exercise addiction. Eating disorders can be as damaging or even more damaging than overeating, and can take a drastic and life-threatening toll on you. Every college has resources to deal with students who are facing a problem with eating disorders – hotlines, support groups, seminars, counseling and medical intervention are just a few of the things many colleges offer. If you suspect that you have an eating disorder, it is vital that you get professional help immediately.

Exercise

An active lifestyle is important to your overall health. Everyone knows they need to stay active, but the majority of Americans fail to make regular exercise part of their lives. "I'm too tired," or "I don't have enough time," are two of the most common excuses. However, the same people who use these excuses seem to find plenty of time to watch television and aren't too tired to attend movies or go to parties with friends. The truth is, if you commit to an active lifestyle, you can find the time and energy to exercise – even during your busy college years.

Why Exercise?

There are plenty of reasons to implement exercise into your daily life. For example, exercise:

- ***Increases your energy*** – it actually makes you less, not more, tired.
- ***Can help you get a better night's sleep*** at the end of the day.
- ***Reduces stress*** and helps "burn off" tension and anxiety.
- ***Is great for overall health***: it reduces your risk of heart disease, high blood pressure and diabetes, and helps to increase bone density.
- ***Increases self-confidence*** and improves self-image.

- ***Makes you look great.***
- ***Is fun*** and contributes to your overall quality of life!

To make healthy activity a regular part of your life:

- ***Develop a realistic exercise plan*** that you can follow.
- ***Set fitness goals*** and maintain a diary of your progress. Keep goals and a diary of your progress in a visible place as a constant reminder of your commitment and success.
- ***Enroll in a physical education class*** to fulfill an elective requirement. Most colleges offer a wide range of physical education classes to fit all kinds of student interests.
- ***Join an intramural sports team.*** It's fun, a great way to meet people, and will help you meet your fitness goals.
- ***Sign up for fitness-focused activities*** through your student activities center. Many colleges organize student ski trips, hiking outings, mountain biking treks and adventure trips at an affordable rate. It's a great way to try out new kinds of activities and meet new people.
- ***Find an exercise partner.*** Having a friend who commits to exercise with you is a great way to stay motivated and stay on track.
- ***Take advantage of your college's resources*** – gyms, fitness classes, personal trainers, activities and organized sports. At no other time in your life will you have access to so many affordable fitness resources – don't let the opportunities pass you by!
- ***Walk or bike to class*** instead of taking the bus or driving. Take the stairs instead of the elevator to your third-floor class. You'd be surprised by what a big difference small changes like these can make to your fitness level.
- ***Choose activity whenever you can.*** Go out dancing with friends at night instead of going to the movies. Walk to your favorite local restaurant for a date instead of opting for delivery. Spend your Sundays playing in a touch football league instead of watching football on TV.

Sleep

There's no doubt about it – managing your time as a new college student is no easy task. And what is the first thing often deleted from the schedule when college students start feeling the pinch on their time? That's right, sleep. Many college students don't think twice about pulling an all-nighter to study, or cutting corners and getting only four or five hours of sleep a night so they can spend more time with friends. But the average college student actually needs between seven and eight hours of sleep every night to maintain optimum health. Are you getting enough?

To Maintain Good Sleep Habits:

- ***Go to bed and wake up at the same time every day.*** Erratic sleep patterns can lead to insomnia and other sleep problems.
- ***Catch a nap.*** Research shows that short naps can actually make you more alert and enhance mental performance. If you feel tired, you are. Take a nap to cope.
- ***Plan well to avoid all-nighters.*** Staying up all night to study is actually counterproductive – you won't absorb much information and will be too tired to perform well on the exam.
- ***Develop a relaxing bedtime ritual*** that will help you sleep. Put on your favorite PJs, read a book, listen to relaxing music or meditate – whatever works for you.
- ***Avoid showers or baths before bedtime*** because they actually stimulate your body. Skip caffeine, alcohol and sleep medications as well – they actually hamper a good night's sleep.
- ***Exercise*** – but not too close to bedtime. Exercise can relax you, setting you up for a good night's sleep. Just make sure you don't get a vigorous workout 30 minutes before you go to sleep.
- ***Design your bedroom to be sleep-friendly.*** Get the temperature right, minimize noise and light, choose comfortable bed linens, and surround yourself with the comforts of home.
- ***If, despite all your efforts, you are still experiencing difficulties sleeping, see an expert.*** Your college physician or other health care professional can ensure that health problems like sleep apnea are not compromising your sleep, and can recommend strategies to help you get the rest you need.

Stress

Stress is an inevitable part of life. In fact, stress can be positive. It can spur you on to action, encourage creativity and enthusiasm, and help you react quickly to dangerous situations. However, if not managed well, stress can cause mental, physical and emotional strain. Left unchecked, out-of-control stress levels can even lead to health problems like anxiety, depression, weight gain, headaches and high blood pressure.

The good news is that we all can implement strategies in our everyday lives to minimize stress and manage it when it does occur. Here's how:

Know When The Stress Is Too Much For You

Your body will give you signs that you are under too much stress. If you find that you are suffering from one or more of the following symptoms, you are probably reaching an unhealthy stress level:

- *Dramatic weight loss or gain*
- *Headaches*
- *Fatigue*
- *Diarrhea*
- *Sleeping too much or having problems sleeping*
- *Muscle tightness or spasms*
- *Frustration, nervousness, irritability and mood swings*
- *Lack of interest in things you used to enjoy*
- *Loss of concentration*
- *Forgetfulness*
- *A feeling of being overwhelmed*

Understand The Common Stressors Of College Life

All college students are different, but most face similar challenges and problems during their college careers. Common sources of college student stress include:

- *Exams and assignments*
- *Grades*
- *Studying*
- *Relationships* – with instructors, roommates, friends, parents, relatives and love interests
- *Time demands and scheduling conflicts*
- *Fear about the future*
- *Finances*

Get A Handle On Stress

You can't eliminate stress from your life. But you can minimize it and its effects. Here are some tips:

- *Practice good organization and time management.* Planning well will help you avoid situations that lead to stress – like forgotten appointments, overdue assignments, lost items, all-night study sessions and projects that leave you pressed for time.
- *Keep your perspective.* Is that one bad grade really the end of the world?
- *Break overwhelming projects into smaller, more manageable tasks.* Instead of cleaning your entire room in one day, for example, set the goal of cleaning and organizing one drawer, one shelf, one area at a time.
- *Stay healthy.* If you are eating well, exercising and sleeping enough, you will be better equipped to handle stress when it comes your way.

- ***Take a break.*** When a situation, project or circumstance is causing you a lot of stress, don't spend long periods of time focusing on it. Take time to think about and do other things, and return when you're ready.
- ***Be positive.*** Every minute you spend panicking and dwelling on the negative is a minute wasted. Instead of beating yourself up for an afternoon about the awful grade you earned on your history midterm, focus on what you can do to ace the final and use your time to develop a plan instead of stressing out.
- ***Relax and have fun.*** No matter how much stress you face, you need to take time for things you enjoy. Schedule exercise, time with friends or family, reading time, or afternoons with nothing to do but shop, catch a movie or visit the park.
- ***Get help if necessary.*** If you become overwhelmed by stress, seek help from a counselor. Sometimes just talking about your stress can help you put it into perspective and get a handle on it.

Illness

College students are especially prone to illness. The stressful, often less-than-perfect college lifestyle, combined with the close contact that students have with each other in dorms and classrooms contribute to the development and quick spread of illnesses. Some, like colds, are little more than an inconvenience. Other illnesses, like hepatitis and meningitis, can be life threatening.

It's probably impossible to complete your entire college career without coming down with an illness at one time or another. But you can reduce your risk by taking the following measures:

- ***Before leaving for college, visit your family physician*** and make sure you have all of the immunizations necessary for college life.
- ***Stay as healthy as possible during college*** by eating right, exercising, getting enough sleep and managing stress.
- ***Cover your coughs and sneezes***, and wash your hands often.
- ***Don't share*** eating and drinking utensils or personal grooming tools like toothbrushes.
- ***Handle food with care.*** Store, prepare and cook foods appropriately. Remember the pizza that sat out all night? It could be full of food-borne pathogens. If you have any doubts about the safety of food, throw it away and eat something else.
- ***Don't overuse antibiotics*** – it can lead to the dangerous development of illnesses that are resistant to antibiotics. Use these medications only

when necessary and only when prescribed to you – never use a friend's leftover antibiotics to self-medicate. If you are prescribed antibiotics, finish the entire course of the drug to ensure that the illness has been cured and won't come back.

- ***See a doctor when necessary.*** Many students put off seeing a doctor and instead pop over-the-counter meds and ignore symptoms. If you are sick for more than a few days or can't seem to get better, see a medical professional to make sure you don't get even sicker.
- ***Avoid unnecessary risks*** like tattoos and body piercing. Unsafe practices during these procedures can lead to infection and spread disease.
- ***Remember safe sex.*** Unfortunately, sexually transmitted diseases (STDs) are very common among college populations. Some STDs are incurable and can lead to death. Abstinence is the only foolproof way to avoid STDs, but if you decide to engage in sexual activity, protect yourself from unnecessary risk.

Depression

Everyone feels sad sometimes and has a bad day now and then. It's part of life's ups and downs. But sometimes feelings of sadness go beyond the normal, healthy range of emotions that we all feel. Depression is a real and serious medical condition – not just something that is "in your head." And, for more than 18 million Americans every year, depression is a condition that affects their mental, emotional and physical health.

College students are particularly vulnerable to depression because of all the life-altering changes they are going through. For the first time, college students may be living away from home, dealing with the stress of everyday life on their own, and facing academic and personal challenges that are new to them.

Depression can be triggered by an event like the loss of a loved one, serious physical illness or injury, a failed relationship, or a series of bad grades. Often, depression is inherited and individuals with a family history of depression may be more likely to suffer from depression themselves. Sometimes depression isn't attributable to any particular cause, but is brought on by a combination of circumstances.

The good news is that depression is a treatable illness. If you are experiencing any of the following symptoms, you should seek help immediately from your college physician or counselor:

- ***Persistent sad, anxious, or "empty" mood.***
- ***Feelings of hopelessness and pessimism.***

- ***Feelings of guilt, worthlessness, helplessness.***
- ***Loss of interest*** or pleasure in hobbies and activities that you once enjoyed.
- ***Decreased energy, fatigue, feeling slowed down.***
- ***Difficulty concentrating,*** remembering, making decisions.
- ***Insomnia, early-morning awakening, or oversleeping.***
- ***Appetite changes*** and/or weight loss, or overeating and weight gain.
- ***Thoughts of death or suicide.***
- ***Restlessness, irritability.***
- ***Persistent physical symptoms that do not respond to treatment,*** such as headaches, digestive disorders, and chronic pain.

Luckily, not everyone will experience depression. But everyone will experience occasional sadness and "feeling down." To help you stay healthy and avoid more serious problems with depression, deal with these feelings positively by:

- ***Staying busy and active*** with things you enjoy.
- ***Creating a support network*** of friends and family.
- ***Making time for yourself*** and the things you value and enjoy.
- ***Taking care of yourself*** by eating well, sleeping enough and exercising.
- ***Avoiding alcohol and drugs.***

If you are like most college students, you probably couldn't wait to get your high school diploma and move on to bigger and better things. And, now that you are experiencing firsthand the excitement and challenges of life as a college student, you are probably experiencing something else, too: homesickness.

It's unavoidable. At some time during all of our lives we will experience homesickness. From our first experience with summer camp, to our years in college, to out-of-state moves for a new job, everyone will, at one time or another, leave the comforts of everything that is familiar for better opportunities, and subsequently feel the pain of homesickness.

Homesickness is natural – and temporary. A little time and a few tried and true techniques are all that you need to overcome homesickness.

This chapter will show you how by:

- Explaining why you are homesick.
- Giving you tips on how to overcome homesickness.

Understanding Homesickness

Homesickness is actually a form of separation anxiety that can occur at any time during a person's life. Young children can experience it on their first days of kindergarten. Teenagers might feel it on their first school trip away from home. Even people well into adulthood often experience this anxiety during times of transition, such as moving for a new job, buying a new home, moving elderly parents into a retirement community or selling their childhood home – or even when they drop off their own grown children at college.

As a new college student, you have left behind the familiar comforts of your home, family and longtime friends and are now experiencing all kinds of new things – people, living arrangements, schedules and routines, expectations – and even food and culture, especially if you have traveled a long way to attend college. Adjusting to all of these changes can be difficult and leave you with feelings of anxiety, sadness, insecurity and even anger. But the feelings of homesickness can be overcome. In fact, in time, the very things that once made you homesick – new challenges, diverse people, different environments – will become the things that inspire you to be excited, passionate and committed to your college career.

Overcoming Homesickness

It takes a little work on your part, but you can minimize feelings of homesickness during this transition period. Here's how:

- ***Meet new people.*** It's as easy as saying "hi" to the person next to you. Remember: most new college students are in the same boat as you, and will welcome a conversation.
- ***Get involved.*** There are lots of activities, clubs, events and causes you can participate in at your college. Follow your interests and develop a healthy social schedule, especially early on when you might be feeling most homesick.
- ***Take a tour.*** Take the time to get to know your surroundings. Grab a map and spend an afternoon exploring the campus and surrounding community. Look for the places and things you will likely need in the future – laundry facilities, restaurants, study nooks, fitness centers, parks, etc. Better yet, ask a new acquaintance, roommate or classmate to come along.
- ***Bring the comforts of home along.*** Just because you're starting a new life in college doesn't mean you have to leave everything behind. Bring some of your favorite comforts along – some pictures to decorate your dorm walls, your favorite comforter for your bed, your music collection, some knick-knacks that remind you of home. The more comfortable you feel in your surroundings, the quicker you will adjust.
- ***Stay healthy.*** If you are feeling awful, exhausted or sick, the first thing you will long for is the comfort of home. Take care of yourself by eating well, controlling stress, exercising and sleeping well so you can focus on the positive aspects of college life.

Chapter 25
Living On Or Off Campus

During your first year of college, most likely you will live on campus. Most colleges recommend that freshman live on campus because it provides a support system and safeguards as students become accustomed to living on their own, away from home. Some colleges even make living on campus during their first year a requirement.

After your first year, however, a variety of living arrangements become available to you – both on and off campus. Before making a decision about your living arrangements during college, there are a few things you should consider.

This chapter will show you how to make an informed and successful choice between on campus and off campus housing by:

- Explaining the differences between on- and off-campus housing.
- Describing the different kinds of housing.
- Outlining the pros and cons of each living arrangement.

On Campus Housing Options

On campus housing is, quite simply, housing that is maintained, operated and subsidized by your college. While most on campus housing is usually physically located on the college campus, some colleges – especially those in urban areas – maintain housing facilities on property that is close to, but not actually part of, the main campus. Common types of on-campus housing include:

Dormitories

The most common type of on campus housing, dorms are usually multi-story buildings featuring individual rooms that are shared by two, or possibly three, roommates. Each dorm floor usually has a kitchen and living area and a suite of bathrooms that are shared by all the residents of a floor. Some newer dorms may include private bathrooms for each room, or bathrooms that are shared by just two or three rooms.

Suites

Suites are like fancy dorms – usually two to four dorm rooms connected by a common living area with a kitchen and shared bathroom. These are kind of like mini-apartments of connected dorm rooms.

Student Apartments Or Townhouses

In recent years many colleges have begun to construct these kinds of on campus housing options, which are basically modeled after the off campus housing that appeals to many students and are just like an apartment or townhouses you would rent, but with the perks of on-campus life. This kind of housing is often only available to upperclassmen, and because of their popularity they can be difficult to secure.

Greek Living

If you choose to join a sorority or fraternity, many of these organizations maintain houses or dormitory floors on campus. Students who choose Greek living live alongside their "brothers," or "sisters" in living arrangements that can range, depending on your college, from luxurious mansion-like homes that contain multiple bedrooms and are maintained by a staff of many, to run-down, overcrowded houses, to a group of dorms alongside each other and assigned to your Greek organization.

Family Housing

Most colleges offer housing specifically designed for students who are married or who have children. Family housing is often similar to student apartments or townhouses, and may include amenities like a day care center, proximity to an elementary school, and playgrounds.

On Campus Housing - Pros & Cons

On campus housing can be a great option for a lot of students, both for their first year of college and the years to follow. But, like everything, on campus living has its advantages and disadvantages:

Pros

- ***Central location.*** On campus housing is usually close to all the things you need – your classes, libraries, campus offices, dining halls, campus recreation and other college resources.

- ***No commute.*** Because you are close to everything, including your classes, you can simply walk out your front door and walk, bike or take a campus shuttle to where you need to be.
- ***Services.*** On campus living often includes convenient services, like cleaning for common areas such as kitchens and bathrooms, trash pick-up, pest extermination, repairs, etc.
- ***Support.*** As a student living on campus, you will have a support network provided by resident assistants and advisors, the campus housing office, campus life and recreation offices, etc.
- ***Cost-effective.*** Once you add up all the services that are included in your housing fees (*meals and utilities, for example*) and subtract the hidden costs of living off campus (*for example, commuting costs and grocery bills – even buying your own toilet paper and cleaning supplies*), the cost of living on campus can be more cost-effective, particularly if your college is in an upscale or urban area.
- ***All-inclusive.*** As an on campus resident, you will not have to worry about bills for heat, air-conditioning, electricity, water, trash or sewer – they are generally included in your housing fee. The only things you may have to pay bills for on a monthly basis are cable or phone service, should you choose to have them.
- ***Safety.*** While crime does occur in on campus housing, this kind of housing generally has more security resources available, including a campus police force, campus surveillance and security systems. It's not always true, but on campus housing can often be safer and more secure than off-campus housing.

Cons

- ***No choice of roommates.*** Many colleges assign you a roommate, giving you little choice of who you will live with. Some colleges do allow student input in the roommate matching process, but you usually are not guaranteed that you will be assigned to your first choice.
- ***Fewer options.*** Depending on your college, you may have a limited list of living arrangements in comparison with off campus options. For example, your college may only offer dorms, while living off campus will give you the option of living in an apartment, townhouses or single-family home.
- ***Limited privacy.*** Shared facilities and group living is part of the on-campus living experience. Many students feel that their privacy is limited while they live on campus. You may even find that the daily buzz of on campus living makes it difficult at times to study, sleep or relax. And if the thought showering in a stall next to your shower-singing roommate or cooking on the same stove as the sloppy neighbor down the hall is unbearable, the appeal of on-campus living might wear thin for you.

- ***Meal limitations.*** In recent years, campus dining has improved greatly, and most colleges offer a broad range of dining options, from health food, to fast food, to late-night dining and food delivery. But many colleges still maintain a dining system of cafeterias that operate on a strict schedule and offer limited food options. If your college only has a few dining options, you may find that living on-campus does not appeal to your culinary tastes.
- ***Rules and regulations.*** To maintain order, protect property and ensure students' safety, colleges enforce a variety of rules in on campus housing, from what kinds of things you can have in your room and how you can decorate your living area, to noise ordinances, curfews and even rules that ban members of the opposite sex from visiting your room except during certain times. Breaking rules can come with consequences, including fines and even eviction. Living under these kinds of rules and regulations can make some students feel that their independence is limited.
- ***Unwelcome visitors and pets.*** Most on campus housing bans pets, and many have rules about how many visitors and what kinds of visitors are permitted. For example, non-students may have to sign in and be escorted while in your dorm, and you may not be permitted to have overnight guests or more than two guests in your room at once.
- ***Parking problems.*** Because parking on most college campuses these days is limited and must be reserved for commuting students, faculty and staff, many colleges issue only a limited number of parking passes for students who live on campus. Some colleges do not allow on campus students to park cars on campus at all, while others may charge high fees for parking permits or grant them through a lottery process on a very limited basis.

Off Campus Housing — Pros & Cons

From renting a room in a local resident's home, to leasing an apartment with a roommate in an apartment complex that caters to students, to renting a home with a group of friends, you will find that there are off campus living arrangements to suit all kinds of students' wants and needs. And, while you may be excited about the prospect of moving out on your own, don't be fooled into thinking that off campus living will be perfect. Just like on-campus housing, off campus housing has its pros and cons.

Pros

- ***It may be less expensive.*** As mentioned before, on-campus housing includes a lot of services and resources – and can be more expensive as a result. But pay careful attention to the costs of living off campus.

The cost of rent may be cheaper, but when you add in the costs of utilities, buying your own groceries, cleaning products and toilet paper, furniture, and commuting, off-campus housing may be as expensive – or more expensive – than living on campus.

- ***It's your choice.*** Off campus housing options are usually plentiful. Depending on where your college is located, you will have a variety of living arrangements to choose from. You can choose a one-bedroom apartment or a three-bedroom apartment, a garden townhouse or a high-rise condo, a house on a plot of land or a private room in a beautiful, historic boarding house. And one of the best things about off-campus living: you get to choose who you live with. You can even choose to live alone.
- ***Space and amenities.*** Off-campus housing is usually more spacious than on-campus housing. And because off campus landlords are competing with each other for your business, many offer lots of perks and amenities to attract tenants. These can include workout rooms, pools, tennis courts, private washers and dryers, and resident social activities.
- ***Privacy.*** When living off campus you can choose a living arrangement that includes a private bedroom and bathroom and, because you are living with just one or a few roommates, rather than an entire dorm of students, it is easier to find quiet time to study, sleep, relax and just be alone.
- ***Independence.*** Because you are making your own choices about where to live, who to live with, how to decorate your living area, and how, in general, to live from day to day, free of the often strict rules of on-campus living, you will probably feel like you have gained independence by moving off campus.
- ***You make your own schedule.*** When living off campus, you don't have to abide by campus dining room schedules, mail pick-up times, curfews, or even closed bathrooms during cleaning. You have your own place – you eat when you want, check your mail when it's delivered, stay out as late as you choose, and clean your bathroom when it's convenient for you.
- ***Plentiful parking.*** This isn't always true – especially if you are living in an urban area – but most off campus housing comes with enough parking spaces to accommodate all residents. Another plus: these parking spaces are usually located in front of your home, not across campus on the long-term parking lot.
- ***Pets – and visitors – are usually welcome.*** While many landlords maintain bans on pets (*or certain types of pets*) or rules about pet ownership, and having a pet may require you to pay an additional fee or deposit, most

students are able to find off-campus housing that allows their furry friends to cohabitate. Off campus housing is more lax when it comes to visitors as well, allowing residents to have overnight guests and multiple guests at one time.

Cons

- ***Less convenient location.*** Moving off-campus means just that – you are moving off-campus, and away from the resources available to you on college grounds. However, since many off-campus housing choices are located just a stone's throw away from campus, you may find that off-campus living is not less convenient – but be sure you think about the inconveniences of your off-campus living option before you make your choice. It may not seem like much, but the longer walks you will be taking to get to the library, the nights you may wake up wishing the all-night cafeteria was just downstairs, or the times you have to drive to the laundromat instead of just walking across the hall, may be enough to make you reconsider living off campus.
- ***More maintenance.*** Living off campus, you will no longer have your bathroom or kitchen cleaned, your furniture repaired, or your room painted on a yearly basis – unless you pay for it out of your own pocket or do it yourself. It's a fact: living off campus often requires more maintenance. And, depending on where you live, your off campus home may require a lot more maintenance. For example, is there a lawn you are required to mow and maintain? If your plumbing becomes clogged, who is responsible for calling – and paying – the plumber? When you see a rodent or a cockroach, will your landlord pay for an exterminator? These are all things to think about before you make the move off campus.
- ***More responsibility.*** With more maintenance comes more responsibility. Remembering to take out the trash, clean out the fridge, and pay the electric bill can be a lot of things to remember as you are meeting the daily challenges of your college career.
- ***Hidden expenses.*** In your off-campus home, there is not a magic fairy that refills the toilet paper every Tuesday like when you lived in the dorm – when you run out of toilet paper, you have to buy more yourself. Off-campus housing seldom comes furnished either, which means you have to buy your own furniture. Add security deposits, groceries, utilities, commuting costs, and cleaning supplies to the mix and you have quite a list of expenses that you may not have thought about before. Make sure you know the costs of living off campus before you sign on the dotted line.
- ***Commuting.*** If your off-campus home is not close to campus, you will have to commute. The added hassle of commuting – whether it is a

20-minute walk, a 20-minute drive, or a 20-minute bus ride to class – is enough to give some students considering off-campus living pause. Make sure you consider how the costs and hassles of commuting will affect your daily life.

- ***Less support.*** Off-campus housing does not come with the support system available through on-campus housing. No longer will you be able to turn to the help of your resident advisor or campus housing office when you have a problem with your roommate or difficulties paying your housing costs. In off campus housing you are basically on your own.

As a new college student, you can probably think of nothing more exciting than getting your first apartment. It's true – moving out on your own for the first time is exciting – but it can also be a time-consuming, frustrating and expensive process.

Don't get taken to the cleaners or settle for a less-than-stellar living arrangement because you are inexperienced and don't understand the apartment rental process.

This chapter will help you make renting your first apartment a good experience by:

- Explaining how to find the right apartment.
- Outlining the important points of dealing with landlords and leases.
- Recommending tips for moving in and out of your apartment.
- Describing special rental circumstances you may encounter.

Finding the Right Apartment

The first step in finding the perfect apartment is defining exactly what you want. Sit down with your chosen roommates and make a list of the features and services that are essential to all of you – those that you would like but don't really need, and the things you would like to avoid. Then set a price range for what you can afford. Some things to think about:

- ***Location.*** You will probably want something close to campus – but should it be within walking distance, biking distance, or just on the public transportation line? Do you want to avoid living on a busy road or near a noisy nightclub? Does proximity to grocery stores, malls, your favorite hangout or your best friend's apartment count?
- ***Safety.*** Sometimes the least expensive apartments are cheap for a reason. Is the apartment you are considering located in a safe neighborhood that is relatively crime-free? Are the units well maintained and up to code? A cheap apartment with an old boiler that could cause carbon monoxide poisoning, with a faulty fire-escape route, or next to an open-air illegal drug market is definitely not worth it – no matter how much money you might save.
- ***Size.*** How many bedrooms do you need? How many bathrooms? Are the rooms large enough to accommodate your furniture, including your computer, drafting table, etc.? Do you need a small yard for a pet? Do you save money by cooking at home a lot and need a kitchen large enough to allow you to cook meals for all your roommates?
- ***Features.*** Every apartment has different features. Which are important to you? Do you go to school in a hot climate and need air conditioning? Are you unwilling to go without a dishwasher or washer and dryer? Will the architectural beauty of a historic apartment building offset the inconvenience of living without air conditioning? Does the newly remodeled kitchen and bathroom justify the added expense?
- ***Amenities.*** What kinds of things can you not live without? A laundry room? Cable television? A security system? A pool or workout facility?
- ***Rules.*** Every landlord and apartment complex has its own rules. Are pets allowed? Parties? What are the consequences of paying rent late? What kinds of noise ordinances are there? Are their certain standards you must maintain, like a clean yard or curtains on the windows? Research the rules and standards and make sure you can live by them.
- ***Furnished or Unfurnished?*** You probably have the option of renting an apartment that comes with basic furnishings or one that requires you to furnish it yourself. Do you need furniture? Are you happy with the furniture that's provided? Is the extra cost of renting a furnished apartment for a year less than the cost of buying your own furniture (*remember you can buy it used or even get it for free from your parents' basement*)?

After you and your roommates agree on the kind of apartment you want, it's time to start looking. Some great places to start include the classified section of the newspaper, the Internet, word-of-mouth, apartment search services, and by simply driving by apartment complexes and buildings you are interested in and checking to see if units are available.

Negotiating with a Landlord and Signing a Lease

Your negotiating power is directly linked to supply and demand. If there are lots of apartments available in your college community, you will most likely be able to leverage a better rental deal. If, on the other hand, quality apartments are difficult to come by in your town, you will have considerably less negotiating power. But don't give up: there are still a few things you can do to negotiate a better rental deal, even if you feel your power is limited:

- ***Sign an extended lease.*** Many landlords would pay to know that their properties are rented to good tenants for the next two years or more. If you love the apartment, have a few years left in college, and feel confident that you will be happy staying there for the long term, consider making the offer to sign a two-year lease in exchange for a reduction in your rent or your security deposit.
- ***Know your rental market.*** Know the going rental rate for apartments in your area and what kinds of amenities and features you can get at that price. Don't be afraid to talk with landlords about what other apartment complexes or buildings are charging and offering, and to inquire why their rates are higher and amenities more limited. You may be able to use the information to negotiate a better rental rate.
- ***Haggle the deposit.*** The deposit is one area where landlords may be willing to make allowances because it will, most likely, be returned to you at the end of your rental agreement. Ask if your deposit can be reduced or, at the very least, paid in increments over several months.
- ***Don't just think money.*** Reducing your rent is ideal, but if that's not possible, ask your landlord to make other allowances, like replacing the flooring, painting, or adding a microwave or new fridge to the deal.
- ***Consider asking for a month-to-month lease.*** Ask your landlord if you can extend your lease on a month-to-month basis once the terms of the original lease are up. This can give you flexibility in the future and help you save on the costs of putting a security deposit down on a new apartment in a year and moving again.

When you have come to an agreement with the landlord about the terms of your rental, don't just sign on the dotted line. The oral agreement you have made with your landlord does not necessarily reflect the lease that he puts in front of you. Before you sign your lease:

- ***Read carefully.*** No matter how boring it is, read every word of the lease and make sure you understand it all. You should even ask if you can take the lease home to review it in private – perhaps with the help of a more experienced friend or family member.

- ***Highlight your concerns and ask for clarification.*** If there is anything in the lease that you do not understand, that you are concerned about, or that you feel was included in error or in contradiction with your oral agreement with the landlord, highlight the section and insist that it is clarified and, if necessary, changed before you put your signature on the dotted line.
- ***Make sure your written lease is identical to your oral agreement.*** During your apartment search process, you made an oral agreement with your landlord or property manager. They may have promised you that the carpet in your specific unit will be replaced before you move in, or that they will waive the pet fee if you move in by a certain date. If your written lease does not reflect these oral agreements, then it is not acceptable. Make sure everything that has been promised to you is in writing in your lease – if it's not then you have no power to ensure your landlord follows through.

Moving In – and Out

Because a rental property is used by multiple people over time, you need to make sure you protect yourself by making note of the condition of the property when you move in – and when you move out. Take the following precautions to protect yourself:

When Moving In:

- ***Conduct a thorough walk- through before moving in.*** During a walk-through, you should inspect every aspect and feature of the apartment and make a detailed list of the imperfections in the apartment. Then present the list to your landlord and ask him or her to sign. Don't overlook holes or stains in flooring or walls, appliances that don't' work properly, light fixtures or outlets that don't function, broken windows or mirrors, bathroom/kitchen cabinets that don't open or close properly, and so on. Once the list has been completed and signed by both parties, keep a copy for yourself.
- ***Make sure it meets your standards.*** If the apartment has not been cleaned, repaired or does not meet the specifications in your lease, inform the landlord and request that the necessary adjustments be made immediately. This is a great reason to request a discount or credit for the delay in your move-in or the inconvenience caused.

When Moving Out:

- ***Conduct a move out walk-through.*** Have your landlord or property manager walk through the apartment with you before you move out so he/she can indicate any potential problems they note, such as damage, changes you have made to the property, or wear-and-tear that goes beyond normal wear and tear, such as floors worn by pets.

- ***Get your landlord to sign off.*** Once you have vacated the property and have brought it up to standards best as you could, have your landlord sign a statement outlining what you will be charged for, if anything, and stating when and how your deposit will be returned to you.
- ***Leave it like you found it.*** It's not only good manners, it makes good sense to leave the property in as good of shape as you received it. First off, you want to establish a good list of references for future rentals – and if your landlord is dissatisfied with you as a tenant he will let your future landlords know, who may charge you inflated security deposits or deny your rental application altogether. Second, leaving a mess or undue damage will cost you – you could forfeit your security deposit and even be charged further fees. Many apartments will charge tenants a minimal cleaning fee (*which should be stated in the lease*) that covers basic cleaning of the property once you have vacated – so the apartment doesn't have to be spotless, but it should be reasonably clean and in good repair.

Special Circumstances

- ***Free-rent promotions.*** To compete, apartment complexes and landlords often design promotional programs to attract and retain tenants. A common promotion is to offer a free month or two of rent, or rent at a significant discount from normal rates. These promotions can be a great way to save money if you can find them and they are legitimate – but read the fine print carefully. To receive the promotional rate, you may have to sign an extended lease, or you may find that the remaining months of rent are inflated in order to make up for the "free" rent you received at the start.
- ***Special discounts.*** Some landlords and property managers offer special discounts to special populations. For example, members or veterans of the military (*and their family members*) may receive a special rental rate, or individuals employed by a specific company or organization may be offered waivers on security deposits or other fees. As you are researching apartments, ask if they offer any special discounts that could apply to you.
- ***Bartering.*** Especially with landlords of smaller properties, you may be able to exchange services for reductions in rent. For example, if you live in a small apartment building located on one acre, you may be able to offer to mow the grass and maintain the landscaping in exchange for $100 off your rent per month. Do you have a summer of working as a house painter under your belt? Let your landlord know that you

would be willing to paint the exterior of the building in exchange for two months of free rent. If you reach an agreement of this kind with your landlord, make sure you develop a detailed and specific written agreement to be signed by both you and your landlord.

- ***Subleasing.*** Because college students are not always able to fulfill the full term of their rental agreement (*a student fails out of college and must move home, for example, or ends up graduating early or transferring to another school*), you may find a variety of subleasing opportunities available to you. Subleasing can sometimes be a good deal because the original leasor is probably in a tight spot and is willing to rent the property to you for less than they are paying, transfer the security deposit to you, or give you furniture or other household goods that they must leave behind. Before you agree to a sublease, however, consider the risks. When you sign a sublease you are most likely assuming responsibility for the property – including damages that may have been caused before you even moved in, or fees and costs that were accrued by the previous tenant. If possible, try to negotiate with the landlord to see if he/she will cancel the previous lease and allow you to sign a new one.

For most college students, living with roommates is part of the college experience – in fact, learning to live with people is quite possibly one of the most important things you will learn during your college years. Some roommates become lifelong friends. Others spend their time living together at each other's throats. You can't control everything – your roommate's snoring, his annoying girlfriend, or love of reality television marathons, for example – but the success of your relationship with your roommates depends largely on you and your ability to negotiate the ups and downs of living with people.

This chapter will show you how by:

- Outlining the traits of a good roommate and showing you how to be one.
- Recommending tips for developing a great relationship with your roommate.
- Suggesting strategies for dealing with difficult roommate situations.

What Makes a Good Roommate?

A relationship with a roommate is the same as any relationship: it takes mutual understanding, a willingness to try to get along, and work. You will find that the people who are easiest and most enjoyable to live with possess some common traits, and you will be a good roommate yourself if you try to develop these characteristics:

- ***An open mind.*** Good roommates accept and appreciate their roommate's individuality – including their culture, religion, family and friends, political beliefs, values, financial situation, intellect, musical tastes, style and appearance.

- ***Respect.*** Good roommates respect their roommate's right to be their own person, as well as their privacy and property.
- ***Responsibility.*** Good roommates take responsibility for their part in the roommate relationship. This includes keeping the living area clean and tidy, paying bills, taking messages, communicating, and performing other duties such as locking the door, getting the mail, or turning off the lights.
- ***Accountability.*** Good roommates are accountable for their behavior, admitting when they are wrong, owning up to mistakes and working to resolve problems. This includes admitting when you borrowed your roommate's sweater without asking or when you forgot to pay the phone bill!
- ***Thoughtfulness.*** Good roommates go beyond the basic responsibilities of living together, and are kind and thoughtful. For example, a good roommate will step out of the room to give their roommate privacy when they are having a personal conversation on the telephone, will wish their roommate good luck on a test, and will remember their roommate's birthday with a card.
- ***Gratitude.*** Good roommates thank their roommate for taking a thorough message or for buying milk, and recognizes when their roommate is especially kind, giving or thoughtful.

Tips for Living with Roommates

Get To Know Your Roommate First

When you are assigned a roommate, it's best to contact him or her before your move-in date, if possible. Many colleges will provide you with the name and contact information of your roommate a month or two before you are scheduled to move in together. Call your roommate to introduce yourself and establish a rapport. Once you feel comfortable, you can begin discussing your living arrangements, including the services you would like to purchase (*cable television, phone service, a rental fridge and microwave, etc.*), the kinds of items each of you should bring (*you bring the television and your roommate can bring the radio, for example*), and the rules that should be established. If you and your future roommate live within a reasonable distance of each other, it can also be a great idea to meet in person before the big move-in day.

Keep An Open Mind

As a new college student, you have probably thought a lot about the kind of roommate you would like. Someone who will become a friend, who enjoys the same hobbies as you, comes from a common background and has similar habits. Don't count on it. College populations are diverse, and the likelihood that you will be matched with someone exactly like you is very small. Don't be disappointed, however. One of the great things about college is meeting new and different people. This will broaden your perspective of the world, your appreciation for people, and your life experience. When meeting your roommate for the first time, keep an open mind and try not to judge or make assumptions. Many college students find that the weird and annoying roommate they encounter on the first day at college quickly becomes a close friend who teaches them a lot and opens their eyes to other ways of looking at the world.

Don't Expect Too Much

On the other hand, don't feel guilty or bad if your roommate doesn't become your best friend. Living with others is difficult, especially for people just getting to know each other, and not every roommate combination will hit it off. Trying too hard to develop a friendship can put a lot of unnecessary pressure on a roommate relationship. Sometimes roommates who live very well together are not particularly close friends, but just fit well as living companions. Getting along with your roommate but not spending all of your time together or developing a close friendship is perfectly acceptable.

Establish Rules

Setting rules will provide structure and a set of common expectations by which you and your roommate can live. Make sure that you and your roommate establish rules together and that you both agree on them. You can also review the rules occasionally and add, delete or revise them to fit your current situation and how it has evolved. Some rules to consider include:

- ***Use of the telephone, television, radio and computer.***
- ***Taking messages.***
- ***Sharing clothes*** and other personal items.
- ***Quiet time*** for studying, relaxing and sleeping.
- ***Cleanliness*** and cleaning duties.
- ***Guests*** – including overnight guests.
- ***Privacy.***

Communicate

Whether you have a great relationship with your roommate or a tenuous one, communication is essential. Letting your roommate know when something is bothering you or when you feel a situation needs attention is the best way to avoid conflict and resentment by resolving problems as they occur. It's also vital that you communicate to your roommate when you are appreciative – for example, thanking your roommate when he washes your dirty dishes or spends extra time at his friend's house so you can have some quiet time alone to study. You may want to set up a regular time each week or so when you and your roommate can talk – meeting for lunch on Wednesdays, for example. If you find that you and your roommate are unable to communicate for any reason, your resident advisor may be able to help you by mediating.

Respect Your Roommate

Every successful relationship begins with respect. Respect for each other's individuality, privacy, property, opinions and values – all of these are the foundation for a roommate relationship that works. Demonstrating respect can be as simple as asking before borrowing your roommate's favorite shirt, or as difficult as respecting your roommate as an individual, despite differences on complex issues like religion, culture and politics. Living with someone very different from you is not always going to be easy – but you will be a better person for it.

Dealing with Difficult Situations

Living With A Friend Or Relative

Living with your best friend or your favorite cousin can sound like a great idea – but sometimes it turns out to be anything but. Don't assume that because you are great friends that you will also make ideal roommates. Sometimes living with someone you already know very well and have a close relationship with can be even more difficult than living with a stranger. If you do decide to go ahead and live with a friend or relative, make sure you treat this living arrangement as you would any other: established expectations and rules, maintain good communication, and respect each other.

Changing Roommates

Sometimes a living situation becomes so unbearable that the problems between roommates can never be resolved. This is when many students consider changing roommates. Some colleges will allow you to change roommates, although you may have to wait until the end of a term or until another living arrangement becomes available. Review your college's policies regarding roommate changes, and contact your resident advisor and campus housing department to find out more. Before taking this action, however, evaluate your reasons for wanting to change roommates and make sure that the situation is truly impossible to resolve.

Living With Roommates Off Campus

Many college students can't wait to move "off campus" to the more independent lifestyle of apartment or rental house living. Getting your first apartment or rental house with a roommate can be a great experience, but there are a few things to keep in mind:

- ***It can be more expensive*** – make sure that you and your roommate can fulfill the financial obligations.
- ***It requires a legal agreement, or lease,*** which makes you legally responsible for the condition of the property and the payment of rent for the term of the agreement. If you and your roommate decide to part ways or become unable to fulfill the lease requirements, you will not be able to just walk away. Getting out of a lease is much more difficult than changing roommates in a campus housing situation. Make sure you know what you are getting into.
- ***It may be more time-consuming*** and involved than taking care of campus housing. There may be a lawn to be mowed, more space to clean and keep tidy, and more utilities to cover – all with no dormitory custodian or campus housing office to help. Make sure you and your roommate have common expectations, and discuss how you will divvy up the additional responsibilities.

Living With More Than One Roommate

If living with one roommate is difficult, then living with two roommates is doubly so (*and three triply!*). At one time or another, most college students will find themselves living with more than one person – in a group house, a multi-bedroom apartment or an on-campus suite, for example. The same rules for living with one roommate apply to living with multiple roommates – respect, rules, communications, etc. – but there are a few additional rules to keep in mind in this specific situation:

- ***Don't gossip or backstab.*** When living with more than one person, it can be easy to fall into the trap of talking about one roommate with another. If there are issues or problems, go right to the source.
- ***Don't gang up.*** Nobody likes to feel like it is them against the world. When there is something that needs to be discussed, be sensitive to your roommate's feelings and discuss it in a calm way – ideally one at a time or in an open group setting, rather than two-against-one.
- ***Be honest.*** When two people live together and someone ate someone else's leftover pizza, it's easy to figure out the culprit. With group living, it's easy to dodge responsibility. If you ate your roommate's pizza or forgot to clean up last night's dishes, don't shrug when asked who did it and suggest that it might have been someone else – own up to what you've done.

Legal Issues

Very rarely, college students will find that the problems of living together become bigger than just annoyances. Unfortunately, in the real world, roommates sometimes steal property and cash, refuse or become unable to pay rent or refuse to do so, destroy property, commit illegal acts like drug use or underage drinking on the shared property, or even threaten or assault their roommates. This isn't something you should spend your time worrying about – but if you suspect or know that your living situation has become dangerous or that your roommate is involved in unlawful activity, you should seek help immediately to avoid further trouble. If you live on campus, your resident advisor or office of campus housing should be able to intervene. In cases of off-campus housing, you may need to seek the help of your landlord, law enforcement or college legal assistance. Most importantly: if you feel you are in immediate danger or that something illegal is occurring, remove yourself from the situation until you can get further help.

According to the Public Interest Research Group, the average annual fee for a regular checking account at a bank is $228. This $228 comes from fees charged by banks for monthly account maintenance, ATM and teller use, automatic bill payment, check writing – the list goes on and on.

You may be tempted to save $228 by stowing your cash under your mattress or in a coffee can under the sink, but that, too, comes with a cost. You won't earn interest on money hidden in a coffee can, and that money under your mattress can be stolen or burned to ashes in a fire.

So what to do? The only real option is to find a bank that offers you the services you want and need, without charging you an arm and a leg.

This chapter will show you how by:

- Helping you choose a bank that makes sense for you.
- Teaching you how to keep track of your account balance.
- Offering you money-saving tips for using banking services.

Choosing a Bank

Banks vs. Credit Unions
Banks and credit unions offer similar services, but differ in whom they serve. Banks want to make a profit for their shareholders, and do so by charging service fees and offering low interest rates on deposits. Credit unions, on the other hand, are nonprofit and owned by the members they serve, allowing them to offer services at a much lower cost while providing higher rates

on deposits than banks. A credit union may seem like the obvious choice, but there are some downsides to this option, including federally mandated membership requirements, a limited number of branches, a smaller network of ATMs and a limited range of services. If you are eligible to join a credit union, it may be a good choice – but weigh your options carefully.

Evaluate Your Banking Needs

To get a complete picture of your banking needs, review your bank statements for the past six months and complete the following chart. If you do not currently have a bank account, estimate your need for these services.

	Month						
Services	**1**	**2**	**3**	**4**	**5**	**6**	**Avg.**
# of Checks							
# of ATM withdrawals							
ATM Fee							
Acctount Maintenance Fee							
Overdraft Fee							
Debit Card Fee							
Low Balance Fee							
Returned Check (NSF) Fee							
Other Fees							

Comparison Shopping

Once you have an idea of your banking needs, you are ready to do some comparison shopping:

- ***Contact several banks in your area*** for information on their services.
- ***Create a chart of their services*** and perform a side-by-side comparison.
- ***Compare the banks' abilities*** to offer services and the fees charged for these services.
- ***Some services you should consider:***

  o Interest Rates
  o Number of ATMs
  o Brokerage Services
  o Insurance Products
  o Direct Deposit
  o Federal Deposit Insurance
  o Online Banking
  o Money Market Accounts
  o Convenience of Locations
  o Loan Services
  o Online Bill Payment
  o Overdraft Protection
  o Credit Card Services

Keeping Track of Your Account

Once you choose a bank, it is essential that you balance your accounts correctly to avoid costly mistakes such as overdrafts and additional fees. Keep track of your accounts with these guidelines:

- ***If you use a debit card, track your usage in a register.***
- ***Use duplicate checks*** so you have copies of your checks for reference.
- ***Write ATM transactions in your register immediately.*** Keep your ATM receipts as a reminder.
- ***Note when you make deposits*** and when the funds will be available. Keep deposit receipts for reference.
- ***Balance your account on a regular basis*** – not just when you receive your monthly statements.
- ***Establish a regular time each week to review your accounts*** and update any activities you may have forgotten.
- ***Set up for online account maintenance*** so you can check your account balances and recent activity any time you want.

Tips to Help You Save

Understand "Free" Checking

Banks used to offer gifts like free toasters to lure new customers. Today's trend is "free" checking. Free checking may appear free on first glance, but banks make a profit by requiring high minimum balances, offering low interest rates and hitting you with a number of hidden fees. Do your research, ask lots of questions and comparison shop to avoid being fooled into paying more for your banking services than you should.

Use Direct Deposit

Processing checks is expensive, so most banks will waive certain fees if you use direct deposit. Ask your employers if they offer direct deposit – and if they do, use it.

Maintain A Minimum Balance

Most banks require you to maintain a minimum balance to avoid additional fees. Banks calculate your minimum balance in one of two ways: daily minimum balance, which requires you to maintain the balance every single day, and average daily balance, which requires you to maintain the balance as an average over the billing cycle. Some banks allow customers to "link" the balances of different accounts, such as a savings account and a checking account, to calculate minimum balances. Understand how your bank calculates your minimum balances, make sure you choose a realistic balance option, and be sure to maintain the balance your bank requires.

Get Overdraft Protection

Sometimes things happen that are beyond your control that cause you to "bounce" a check – at the cost of around $25 per check. For example, you might write several checks to pay bills, and then find out that your student loan or scholarship funds were never deposited due to an accounting error. This is why overdraft protection is a must. With overdraft protection, banks advance you the money to cover the checks you have written, allowing you to avoid overdraft fees. In most cases this is a free service, although interest may be charged on the money that was advanced to you.

Ask for Discounts and Waived Fees

Once your bank has you as a customer, they want to keep you. Don't be shy about asking your bank for a better deal or to waive certain fees.

Be Smart About Using Services

To reduce fees:

- ***Know where your bank's "no-fee" ATMs are located.*** Most banks' ATMs charge non-customers a fee for their use – an average of $1.40 per transaction, according to Bankrate.com's most recent survey of checking accounts. Avoid these fees by using your own bank's ATMs.
- ***Request cash when you use your debit card to avoid ATM fees.*** Most banks don't charge fees for debit card use.
- ***Limit transactions and bank visits*** to avoid going over the maximum transactions you are allowed per month.

Don't Order Checks From Your Bank

Most banks charge between $12 and $17 for a box of 250 checks. A cheaper option? Order checks directly from the check-printing company. Find these companies on the Internet, in the weekend newspaper, and through offers that come in the mail. Many offer discounts for first-time customers, so consider changing companies each time you order checks.

Consider Using Online Banking

Online banking is a safe and convenient alternative to traditional banking. Because it is cost-effective, banks encourage customers to take advantage of this service by offering incentives and waiving fees.

- Helping you choose a bank that makes sense for you.
- Teaching you how to keep track of your account balance.
- Offering you money-saving tips for using banking services.

It's an old cliché: the starving student who survives for months on macaroni and cheese and brings his laundry home to mom to get it done for free. It doesn't have to be that way. In fact, between student grants and loans, savings, parental contributions and part-time jobs, most students have enough money to live well – they just don't know how to budget and make their money last.

Most financial experts agree that the most important step to financial freedom and success is creating a budget. But many people, especially students, don't do this. A good budget, combined with some smart money-saving tips will help you survive your college years in good financial shape.

This chapter will show you how by:

- Showing you how to create a budget that works.
- Outlining strategies to deal with budget problems.
- Recommending tips for making your budget stretch as far as it can go.

A Budget that Works for You

A lot of people have negative feelings about the word "budget." When they think of budgeting, they think of depriving themselves, strict discipline and cutting out luxuries. But, if you think about it, the opposite is true – a budget is actually a blueprint for living well and in the manner you would like on the money you have.

In the long run, a budget actually empowers you to have the things you want by giving you a true picture of your financial situation and helping you understand the actions you need to take to achieve the financial milestones you want – whether its taking a vacation during spring break, buying a new car after graduation, or purchasing your first home by the time you are 25.

So what are you waiting for? Creating a personal budget that works for you not only helps you to survive now, on a student budget, but it will also put you in the position to achieve financial freedom and success for a lifetime. Here's how:

Calculate How Much Money Is Coming In

It's a no-brainer: to understand how much money you have to spend and how you should spend it, you need to have a solid picture of how much money you have coming in. This includes money from scholarships, loans and grants, parents, jobs, investments, savings – anything you earn or receive money from. Use the following simple chart to organize your monthly income:

Monthly Income

Source	Amount/Month
Gross salary (before taxes/deductions)	$1545
Part-time job	$575
Interest from savings	$35
TOTAL	
Average/Month	

Calculate How Much Money Is Going Out

Now it's time to figure out where your money goes. Collect all your bills and receipts for a month or two, then sit down with paper or pen and make an honest list of how you spend your money. Don't leave anything out! Here are some expenses you probably have:

- ***Housing.*** Whether you rent or pay a mortgage, this is probably the largest expense on your list. Even if you're still living at home, perhaps you're contributing some money to your parents.
- ***Utilities.*** All the things we take for granted – like electricity, water, gas, phone, cell phone and garbage collection – fall into this category. Gather the receipts you've paid over the past few months and you'll have a good idea of how much these expenses cost.

- ***Debt Service.*** Probably the second-largest category in your list of expenses is repayment of debts. Include payments on everything for which you owe money: student loans, car payments, credit cards, etc.
- ***Insurance.*** Auto, health or renter's – all the insurance you pay for.
- ***Taxes.*** Analyze your paycheck and any other documents that identify the amount of taxes you pay. Includes items like state, federal, Social Security and Medicare taxes. You may find it helpful to review your past state and federal income tax returns to calculate a monthly total to determine if you are contributing the correct amount to your tax bill each month.
- ***Transportation.*** This includes all expenses you pay to keep your car working, like gas, oil changes and repairs. In addition, include in this category items like tolls, licensing/registration fees, and vehicle inspections. If you routinely use public transportation, like the bus or subway, include that amount in this category.
- ***Entertainment.*** This may be another big category. Include everything you do for fun – movies, vacations, eating out (*yes, include those Big Macs*), concerts, Internet access, the double latte you have every morning, the clubs you go to on weekends. Everything. Don't forget books, CDs, DVDs (*either bought or rented*), cable TV. If the expenses in this category are quite large, you might consider breaking it up into smaller categories like "eating out" and "vacations."
- ***Personal.*** Food, clothing, shoes, dry cleaning, health club fees, haircuts, manicures, make-up, pet care – expenses like these make up this category.
- ***Contributions.*** List any money you contribute to charities or other organizations.

Divide Your Expenses Into Fixed Expenses And Variable Expenses

There are two kinds of expenses: fixed expenses, which are expenses that occur regularly and usually in the same amount, like rent and utilities; and variable expenses, which are expenses that vary in frequency and amount, like groceries and entertainment costs. Organize your fixed and variable expenses in the following ways:

Sometimes fixed expenses occur every month (*rent, fitness club dues*), but some are paid annually or quarterly, like car insurance. Because they happen regularly and the amounts don't change, it should be easy to list your fixed expenses. Checks you've written should be listed in your check register – you can get the amounts from there. Or gather up the receipts from the last few months' bills and take the numbers from there. Assign your monthly expenses to the appropriate day of the month on which they normally occur. Assign your yearly expenses to the month of the year they occur.

Monthly Fixed Expenses

1 Ex: Rent $550	12	23
2	13	24
3	14	25
4	15 Ex: Cable $35	26
5	16	27
6	17	28
7	18	29
8	19	30
9	20	31
10	21	
11	22	**Monthly Total:**

Yearly Fixed Expenses

January	
February	
March	Ex. Car Registration $380
April	
May	
June	
July	
August	
September	
October	
November	
December	Ex. Holiday Gifts $200
TOTAL	
Monthly Average	

Because they change, variable expenses are a little more difficult to determine. You could estimate them, but avoid the temptation to do this because you will probably vastly underestimate the amount you spend. Here's a surefire way to nail down what you're spending: write down every penny you spend for a month. It's easy – just carry a small notebook with you to enter the cost of everything you buy. You'll probably be astonished at where your spare cash goes – most people are. Other things you can do include:

- ***Write a description of the purchase for each check you write.***
- ***Keep all the receipts from credit card purchases*** and write the purpose of the expense on the back of the receipt.
- ***Record your daily spending*** in a spreadsheet or on a chart.
- ***Once a week, review your daily expenses and total them.*** The results are likely to be a big surprise!

After you've collected a month's worth of variable expenses, you should be in a better position to determine how much you spend for each kind of variable expense. If you want to be even more accurate, continue collecting daily spending records for another two months.

The following chart is an example of how you can record your variable expenses. You will notice that there is a section for credit card expenses – use it only if you are currently paying off previous credit card balances. If you purchase items during the month with your credit card that would be classified as variable expenses, list those in the appropriate category. For example, if you purchase $40 worth of groceries with your credit card, enter that amount in the Groceries section.

Monthly Variable Expenses

Expenses	Week 1	Week 2	Week 3	Week 4	Totals
Transportation					
Household					
Snacks					
Entertainment					
Laundry					
Groceries					
Personal Care					
Utilities					
Credit Card					

Keep using this chart as many times as you want – and change the expense categories to fit your circumstances. Just be sure to keep track of everything!

Create An Income Statement
Here's where you figure out whether you have enough money in your budget to cover what you spend. Simply transfer the information you gathered from the previous pages into the following chart, called an income statement:

Income Statement

Monthly Income	
Minus Monthly Fixed Expenses	
Minus Yearly Fixed Expenses (*Monthly Average*)	
Minus Monthly Variable Expenses	
Remaining Income	

Budget Problems

After laying it all out on paper, you now have a solid picture of your financial status. But you may find that your budget is anything but balanced. What should you do now? Some problems you may encounter include:

Having More Expenses Than Income
Unfortunately, this is the most common student budget problem. When you find that you have a negative number in the Remaining Income column of your income statement, then you are spending more money than you have. One solution to this problem is to earn or bring in more money – but this isn't always possible. The other option is to cut spending.

Before you get upset, you should realize that cutting spending doesn't always have to mean depriving yourself or eliminating luxuries entirely. Perhaps you can cut your expenses by eating out one time a week rather than three. You can even turn this cost-cutting into something fun, by using eating in as an opportunity to learn how to cook. Renting movies Friday nights with friends can become a low-cost but fun ritual that replaces the more expensive habit of going out to clubs.

Take a look at your fixed expenses as well as your variable expenses. Could getting a roommate cut your living expenses significantly? Do you really use your gym membership, your HBO subscription, or all the features of your phone service, like voice mail and caller ID?

Taking a long, hard, honest look at how you spend your money can go a long way toward getting your budget in balance. You'll need to cut expenses until the Remaining Income row of your income statement has a positive number. Remember – just breaking even isn't enough. You'll need some money left over every month to cover unexpected costs, like your car breaking down or your computer needing repairs. For more cost-cutting ideas for living on a student budget, check out the tips in the next section.

Having More Income Than Expenses
This is a great problem to have! If you find that you have a positive number in your Remaining Income row, then you are living within your means – congratulations! Now you must create a plan for what to do with your remaining income and stick to it so your valuable income doesn't slip away. Think about your financial goals – would you like to pay off your debt, save for a vacation, replace your car when you graduate, open up a retirement account? Make a list of your long- and short-term financial goals, then figure out how you can use your remaining income to achieve these milestones.

Budget Maintenance
The biggest problem that most students encounter with their budget is simply that they don't stick to it! Some students fail to curb impulse spending and continue to exceed their budget on a monthly basis. Other students don't revise their budget regularly to reflect changes in circumstances – like the loss of income when they quit their part-time job, or the addition of an expense when they are prescribed a fairly expensive allergy medicine.

Once you have developed a budget, don't let all your hard work go to waste. Creating a budget is not a one-time activity, but an important part of your overall financial routine you need to maintain for the rest of your life. Any time something changes in your life – like getting a better job, marrying, moving to another state – you should reevaluate your budget. However, you should retool your budget every few months, even if there haven't been any major changes in your life.

Budget-Saving Tips

Listed below are a few great methods to help you survive on a student budget:

- ***Cut coupons.*** You probably think of suburban moms and old people when you think of cutting coupons, but you shouldn't. Coupons are a great way to save money – and why pay more for something if you don't have to? If you're worried about the time it takes to find and cut coupons, surf the Internet for them – company Web sites often offer possible coupons for their products. And there are even Web sites designed to give their audience tips on where to find the best coupons. Keep a file where you put coupons you find for restaurants, movies and other entertainment, groceries, toiletries and services, then refer to the file every time you need to make a purchase to see if you have a coupon.

- ***Shop sales.*** There's absolutely no reason to pay full price for anything because just about everything goes on sale eventually. When you see something you can live without – a great pair of shoes, for example – discipline yourself to wait and watch. Eventually those shoes will go on sale. After holiday sales, end-of-the-season sales and going-out-of-business sales are great ways to find what you need and want for less.
- ***Comparison shop.*** It takes more time, but when you want or need to make a purchase, don't buy what you want at the first place you find it. Check out store circulars, browse the aisles and use the Internet to find out who is offering the lowest price and the best deal on the things you need and want.
- ***Ask and ye shall receive.*** Sometimes all you have to do is ask. Call your credit card company and ask for a lower interest rate or to have a fee waived. Ask your bank to remove a specific fee.
- ***Find freebies.*** College life is full of freebies, if you know where to look. For example, you could probably get a great, free lunch at least once a week if you keep your eyes open for grand openings of restaurants, promotional barbeques, and campus club membership drive parties that offer free food. Companies often use groceries stores in campus locations to market and promote new products, and give out free samples of everything from bars of soap to sample sizes of laundry detergent to six packs of the latest energy bar.
- ***Exploit your student status.*** They may not advertise it, but a lot of businesses offer discounts to students. Movie theaters usually have cheaper student ticket prices, local restaurants may offer a 10 percent discount to college students, and grocery stores in campus areas often choose a day of the week as "student savings day" and offer a discount to student shoppers. You'll never know about these offers if you don't ask, so bring your student ID card everywhere you go and ask if they offer a student discount.
- ***Spend to save.*** Sometimes you have to spend money to save money. For example, spending $30 every three months to change your car's oil is costly, but not as much as having to replace your car's engine when it runs out of oil and burns up because you haven't paid for an oil change for over a year. Regular tune ups for your car can help it run more efficiently, reduce fuel costs. Regular trips to the dentists can help prevent costly – and painful – problems with your dental health. In the long run, maintenance is far less expensive than fixing problems that arise from neglect.
- ***Live simply.*** Sometimes simplifying your life is the best thing you can do to preserve your finances – and your sanity. There are lots of little things you can do to reduce your costs – and improve the overall quality

of your life in the process. Consider canceling cable television and listening to music or reading instead. You'll save money and discover that you enjoy time spent without the buzz of the TV. Stop buying the newest fashions every season, and instead stick to a few classics. You'll save tons and probably find you appreciate that fewer choices makes it easier to get dressed in the morning!

- ***Borrow.*** You don't have to own everything – you can borrow or share probably half of what you need. Bored of your wardrobe? Borrow a sweater or some accessories from roommates, or have a clothing swap with a group of friends. Only need a car occasionally? Make a deal with your roommate to contribute to gas and maintenance costs if he lets you use his car once a week for a few hours. Borrow books, movies and CDs from the library instead of buying them or renting them. Ask your mother if you can borrow her camera for spring break instead of buying one for yourself. Thinking about getting a dog or buying a motorcycle? Offer to take care of your friend's dog for the weekend and consider renting your dream motorcycle from a dealership for a few hours to find out what ownership might really be like before making the commitment to buy. Just make sure you treat the items you borrow with respect and return them in the same condition you borrowed them in.
- ***Wait before you buy.*** One of the biggest things you can do to stick to a student budget is to completely eliminate impulse buying. When you see something you want, resolve to wait 48 hours before making the purchase. More often than not you will find that you forget about the item, decide you don't really want or need it, or find something you want even more at a better price. If, after 48 hours, you still feel you can't live without it, figure out how to pay for it and make the buy. You'll find that you end up making purchases that you truly appreciate and don't regret, and will end up making fewer purchases overall.
- ***Brush up on frugal living.*** There are entire books, magazines and Web sites dedicated to helping people live on less. Go to the library, browse the newsstands and search the Internet regularly for ideas on saving money and sticking to a budget.

As a college student, you will be inundated with credit card offers. Representatives from credit card companies will beckon from kiosks on campus, offering you free t-shirts and beach towels in exchange for your credit card application. Enticing offers – some with actual credit cards in your name enclosed – will arrive in the mail. Commercials on TV, radio, billboards and in magazines and newspapers will promise you convenience and benefits if you carry their card in your wallet.

Credit cards are necessary, and sometimes even a great option – but they are not "free money." Using credit cards will be necessary during your life, but abusing credit cards is something to be avoided at all costs.

This chapter will help you understand credit cards, use them well, and avoid their pitfalls by:

- Describing the pros and cons of credit cards.
- Outlining which credit cards might be best for you.
- Recommending strategies for using credit cards wisely.

Understanding Credit Cards

Most financial experts agree that adults should carry at least one credit card. That said, the rate at which college students acquire, use and abuse credit cards has risen to alarming rates over the last decade. Credit cards are necessary, but because they can also get you into financial trouble that can take years to resolve, you should make sure you understand the pros and cons of credit cards before you sign on the dotted line for the first time.

Pros

- ***Security.*** Credit cards give you the ability to make payments when cash is not available and checks are not accepted. For example, if your car breaks down on a dark highway while you are traveling cross-country, chances are you won't have sufficient cash to pay for repairs, and that mechanic in the middle of nowhere is unlikely to accept your personal check. That's when your credit card comes in handy. Traveling is also safer when you can avoid carrying large amounts of cash, and little emergencies always seem to come up in life when cash is in short supply.
- ***Establishing credit.*** As a young adult, you have the opportunity to begin building a credit history, which will be used by everyone from employers to insurance companies to lenders to get a better picture of your financial character and dependability. Having good credit is vital – and credit cards are an important part of building good credit. Receiving a credit card from a major credit card company and using it responsibly is a great way to establish good credit.
- ***Flexibility.*** If used wisely, credit cards give you a little flexibility in your budget. For example, perhaps you absolutely have to have a new pair of running shoes today to participate in the 5K charity race this weekend, but you don't have the extra money in your budget until next month. Using a credit card to purchase the shoes and then paying of the balance when you receive your statement is a great way to delay payment for a few weeks until you can find the room in your budget to pay off the purchase. That said, if you don't pay off the credit card balance as you planned, you will end up paying more for the shoes than you budgeted – negating all the benefits of using the credit card to begin with.
- ***Rewards.*** Some credit cards offer rewards such as points, airline miles, cash back or prizes. These rewards can be great little perks – however, they are seldom a good reason to accept a credit card. Think of credit card rewards as icing on the cake – not the main reason to order the card.

Cons

- ***You pay to use.*** Believe it or not, credit card companies don't give you credit out of the goodness of their hearts. They make money off the process – lots and lots of money. If you use credit cards you will pay fees, interest, and service charges. That is, unless you are absolutely and perfectly meticulous with your credit card use, chances are you will eventually pay the credit card company at least something. Which is fine if you are willing to pay for the benefits that credit cards afford you – but it can be devastating if you let your credit card use get out of control.

- ***Temptation.*** Having a credit card in your wallet is like having a little devil on your shoulder. If you're not careful, that little devil can talk you into making a lot of purchases you can't afford. You have to see credit cards for what they really are – loans – not for what you wish they were – free money. Sure, you can have anything you want by purchasing it on credit, but you will be paying for it for a long, long time.
- ***Credit can cloud your financial picture.*** To survive on a student budget, you have to have a clear picture of your financial situation. Having a credit card can cloud that important picture if you allow yourself to believe that your credit card debt doesn't count, or if you start to consider the available balance on your credit card as part of your income or available funds.

What Kind of Card is Best for You?

To pick the best credit card for you, you should make a list of cards available to you and compare the benefits and features of each card. The card that provides the best benefits and features for your lifestyle is the one to apply for. But, to pick the best card, you must fully understand the ins and outs of credit cards. Here are a few clues:

Annual Fees

Some, but not all, credit cards charge annual fees. Often, the cards that charge these fees offer valuable benefits to cardholders, such as insurance coverage. Sometimes the credit cards offered to people with no credit or bad credit charge annual fees to offset the costs of possible customer default. As a student, you should choose a card that does not charge an annual fee – there are plenty of them out there and you should be able to find one that will extend credit to you.

Interest Rates

Interest rates are the rates credit card companies charge you to "borrow" or "use" the money you spend on their card. Interest rates vary wildly and can depend on your credit score and benefits offered by the card. The interest rate on you credit card really doesn't matter if you pay off the balance of the card every month. But chances are there will be times when you will need to carry a balance, so you should try to find a card with the lowest rate possible.

Insurance

Many credit cards offer card members insurance coverage on the things they purchase on the card. Insurance specifics vary from card to card, but generally these insurance policies cover things like theft, damage or fraud. If you plan on making several important, expensive or large purchases on your credit card, insurance policies like these can be a great benefit.

Free Stuff
You can get everything from t-shirts and telephones to free gas and airline tickets in exchange for your acceptance and use of a credit card. Free stuff is great, but make sure that the freebies don't trick you into accepting a card that doesn't offer you the services you need, or has unnecessary fees or high interest rates.

Membership Or Special Interest Cards
Just about every group has a credit card these days. You can get credit cards with your college mascot on it, credit cards that declare you a fan of a sports team, and credit cards that pledge your commitment to a variety of issues and causes. These cards sometimes come with benefits – like discounts on team merchandise or a percentage of your purchases going toward the issue of your choice.

Credit Card Programs
After you've had your credit card for a while, you will begin to receive marketing calls offering you "special" programs available only to card members. These special programs can include travel clubs, insurance that covers your credit card payments should lose your job or have health problems, and identity theft protection plans. While these programs can sound like a great idea, they usually come with a hefty fee that is added directly to you credit card balance, and seldom offer benefits that you can't find elsewhere for less – or for free.

Now that you have an understanding of the credit card world, it's time to pick the one that's right for you. You can make it easier for yourself by using one of the online credit card comparison Web sites, like www.creditcards.com. Sites like this lay out the terms and benefits of a variety of credit cards so that you can see and compare, in black and white, just what the cards you are considering offer.

Avoiding Problems

Again, the point of carrying a credit card is to build your credit and give yourself flexibility and security – not to get yourself in financial trouble. Make sure you avoid the credit card pitfalls common to college students by implementing the following strategies:

Keep Just One Card
There is absolutely no reason for a college student to have more than one credit card. If you currently have more than one, consolidate your balances to the card with the lowest interest rate and cancel the others.

Set A Limit
Even if your card offers you a $5,000 limit, you don't have to accept it. Call your credit card company and instruct them to set your limit at a level you are comfortable with. If you are concerned that you may have problems maintaining discipline with your credit card, select a card that requires you to pay off your balance at the end of every month, such as an American Express card.

Get A Great Interest Rate
If you already have a credit card but are not satisfied with your interest rate, call the company and ask them to lower it. If they know you are considering canceling your card or consolidating additional debt to their card, they may be willing to give you a better rate.

Keep Track
Throughout the month, keep track of the purchases you make on your credit card so you know how much you will need to pay off when the balance statement comes. Unless you write down your purchases, it will be easy to forget or overlook the purchases you make.

Use – Don't Abuse
Using credit cards helps build credit, but abusing them can destroy it. If you find that your credit card use is getting out of control, stop using them until you can pay off the debt. Cut up the cards, freeze them in ice, or ask a trusted friend to hold on to them until you get the situation under control.

Avoid Late Fees
Paying late fees is just stupid. Even if you are only able to make the minimum payment, make some kind of payment on time to avoid the fees – which can be as high as $30 or more. If you find that your bill is due at an inconvenient time of the month or you have forgotten to make a payment that is due today, call the credit card company. They may be able to change your billing due date or take a payment over the phone by using your checking account to help you avoid a late fee.

Maintain Good Credit
Whatever you do, don't let your credit card use damage your credit. Keep your purchases under control; use only one card, budget well, and contact the credit card company if you are having problems making payments. Credit card companies want their money – and will usually make allowances to help you pay off your debt.

When it comes to credit, someone is always watching. It's not as sinister as it sounds, and it isn't a plot line in some "Big Brother Is Watching You" science fiction story. Quite simply, every time you do something to affect your credit – sign up for a new credit card, make a late payment, accept a line-of-credit increase – it is recorded in a report that is read by a variety of people who can impact your lifestyle, including lenders, landlords, and even employers.

Do you know what your credit report says about you? If not, you should. As a college student, the decisions you make when it comes to credit will affect you for years to come, and could impact your ability to have the things you want in life, like a good job, a comfortable home and a great car.

This chapter will help you understand credit reports by:

- Explaining what a credit report is.
- Outlining the reasons why your credit report is important to your life.
- Letting you know how to get a free copy of your credit report.
- Describing how to maintain a good credit report.

What is a Credit Report?

Several companies called credit bureaus compile and maintain a database of individual credit reports that are provided to interested parties on request. These credit reports look very much like a college transcript, and contain a detailed history of your borrowing and payment habits for the past seven to ten years. More specifically, your credit report includes:

- ***Personal information.*** Including your name, telephone number, current and previous addresses, Social Security number, date of birth, and current and past employers.
- ***The story of your credit.*** Seven years of your history, including accounts opened and closed, credit amounts, payments made, late payments to banks, credit cards, retailers and lenders.
- ***Public records.*** Other financial information including personal bankruptcies, debts owed to tax agencies, and court judgments against you.
- ***Inquiries.*** Every time you try to obtain credit or give someone permission to access your credit report, it is noted on your report. The length of time these remain on your report varies.
- ***Current credit.*** All the info on your current credit accounts, including amounts owed, credit available, and payment amounts on installment loans.

According to federal law, credit bureaus are allowed to give your credit report to the following parties:

- ***Creditors*** who are considering giving you or have given you credit.
- ***Employers*** considering you for employment, promotion, reassignment, or retention.
- ***Insurers*** considering you for an insurance policy or reviewing an existing policy.
- ***Government agencies*** reviewing your financial status or government benefits.
- ***Anyone else with a legitimate business need for the information***, such as a potential landlord.
- ***Parties who have a court order or federal jury subpoena*** for your credit report.
- ***A third party*** to whom you have requested, in writing, that your credit report be issued.

There are two kinds of inquiries made regarding your credit. "Hard" inquiries are made when you seek to obtain credit, or when you authorize someone to access your full credit report. "Soft" inquiries are not a request for your full credit history, but instead requests for general information, usually when a company is gathering marketing information about potential customers – like when a credit company creates a list of people to send credit card offers to. When you request a copy of your own credit report, it is also considered a soft inquiry.

Credit reports are not the same as credit scores. While a credit report is a detailed history of your borrowing and payment habits, your credit score is a number assigned to you based on your history that indicates the financial risk you pose to lenders. Much like your grade point average, which is used to create a quick portrait of your academic achievements, your credit score is a quick and easy number based on financial facts that gives lenders a picture of how desirable – or risky – you would be as a customer.

Why is My Credit Important?

Although your credit report and your credit score may seem like just a few more statistics or abstract figures – and ones that are irrelevant to your daily life – nothing could be further from the truth. You will find that the strength of your credit can affect everything from how much you pay for services, to what kind of home you can afford, to whether you will receive that big promotion or not. Here are just a few things that credit can affect:

Insurance Rates
Believe it or not, many insurance companies use credit scores to decide whether to offer a customer car insurance, and how much to charge them for insurance. Insurance companies do this because reliable studies indicate that the lower a person's credit score, the higher the probability that that person will incur losses on an automobile insurance policy, and the higher the expected loss on the policy. If you do not have a strong credit score, you may end up paying more for car insurance, or even be denied insurance.

Interest Rates On Loans And Credit
It makes sense: the riskier you are as a credit customer, the higher the rate a lender will charge to defray the potential costs of you defaulting on a loan. If your credit report indicates that you are a credit risk, you will be charged considerably higher interest rates on credit cards, mortgages, car loans and installment loans.

Your Ability To Secure A Mortgage, Car Loan Or Business Loan
If your credit report indicates that you are a considerable credit risk, you may be denied credit, no matter how high an interest rate you are willing to pay. Being denied credit like mortgages, car loans, business loans, and student loans can prevent you from achieving goals and fulfilling dreams like owning the perfect home, starting your own business, pursuing an advanced academic degree, or purchasing the car you need to travel to and from your dream job.

Your Employment
Some employers use credit history information simply to decide if a job candidate is responsible and reliable, or just to confirm identity. Other employers are concerned about hiring applicants whose credit reports

indicate they cannot manage their financial affairs, or whose monthly debt payments are too high for the salary offered for the given position. Employer credit inquiries are often limited to management and executive positions, or to positions that give applicants access to cash, assets, a company credit card, or confidential information. If a potential employer wishes to obtain your credit report, you must give them permission, often in the form of a waiver or form you sign during the application process. If your credit report is the reason you are turned down for employment, by law the employer must let you know and give you time to review your report and respond. Even if you are already employed, your employer may require a credit inquiry before granting you a promotion, security clearance, access to corporate funds or reassignment to another department or position. If your credit report indicates that you are not a dependable bill payer, that you are overextended financially, or that you have a number of serious delinquencies, employers may deem you undependable, unstable and a risky employment candidate.

Your Ability To Rent An Apartment

Landlords routinely acquire the credit reports of potential tenants in order to assess whether the tenant is able and likely to pay rent in a timely manner. When trying to rent an apartment, expect a credit inquiry to be part of the application process.

Free Credit Reports

A recent amendment to the federal Fair Credit Reporting Act requires each of the nation-wide consumer reporting companies (*Equifax, Experian, and TransUnion*) to provide youwith a free copy of your credit report, at your request, once every 12 months.

Because this is a new program, it is being introduced in phases. However, everyone will have access to free credit reports by September 1, 2005. To learn more about the free credit report program, visit the Federal Trade Commission's Web site at www.ftc.gov.

If you are not currently eligible for a free credit report and you need one, by all means purchase one. The fee is minimal – less than $10 – and taking action now maysave you from a lot of problems in the future.

You can obtain a free copy of your credit report from the following major credit bureaus:

Equifax	**Experian**	**TransUnion**
(800) 685-1111	(888) 397-3742	(800) 888-4213
www.equifax.com	www.experian.com	www.transunion.com

Maintain Your Credit Report

Now that you know how important your credit report is to your life and how to get a free copy of your credit report, how do you go about maintaining a credit report that accurately reflects who you are? Just as you must establish a sensible exercise routine to maintain good physical health, you must establish a regular routine to check on your credit report and correct any discrepancies you may find. Here's how:

Check In Regularly
Experts agree that everyone should review their credit reports from the three major credit bureaus on a yearly basis. It is important to obtain reports from all three bureaus – these bureaus operate independently and could possibly have very different information about you. If you regularly check your report, you may be able to catch mistakes and fraud – like identity theft – early, and minimize damage.

Look Before You Leap
Requesting a copy of your credit report before making a big financial decision is also a great idea. To avoid unpleasant surprises, get a copy of your report when you are:

- ***Applying for a major loan,*** like a mortgage.
- ***Applying for a job.***
- ***Going through a major life change,*** like marriage or divorce.
- ***Denied credit.***

Look For Mistakes
Pay attention to every detail on your credit reports, and take special note of anything that seems inaccurate. Even though a credit report seems official, don't be intimidated into believing that if it is in black and white on the report it must be true. You know your credit history better than anyone, and if you feel something is suspicious or wrong, it probably is. Mistakes on your credit report can indicate something as simple as a clerical error by a creditor or the bureau, or something as serious as identity theft.

Make A Claim
By law, credit bureaus are required to investigate any claim about credit errors within 30 days. When a bureau receives an error claim, it forwards the claim to the creditor in question. If it is determined that an error has been made, the bureau must correct the error, notify the other bureaus, and send you a free report to prove that the error has been corrected. To make a claim:

- ***Document the claim in writing.***
- ***Inform the creditor in question yourself.***

- ***Send documentation such as cancelled checks or statements,*** but always send copies. Keep originals for yourself.
- ***Keep and record all correspondence between you, the bureau and the creditor,*** including e-mails and phone calls. Include dates and names.

Make Your Voice Heard
If a bureau refuses to acknowledge an error, but you still believe an error has been made, you can add a short statement to your credit report that explains your side of the story. This statement will be sent along with your credit report to anyone who requests your credit history in the future, and will also be sent to anyone who has requested your credit history in the recent past.

Dealing With Bad Credit
Sometimes a bad credit report is not the result of errors on the part of the bureau or creditors, but a result of mistakes you have made. Many college students find themselves in the unfortunate situation of being overwhelmed by debt. If this happens to you, it is critical that you take swift action to correct your mistakes and turn your problem around. One option is to enlist the help of credit counseling services.

Credit counselors help consumers understand their credit problems, change the behaviors that led to their problems and take the steps necessary to repair their mistakes and improve their credit report and score. Be warned, however: there are many so-called credit counseling firms that do everything but help you, and will charge you exorbitant fees in the process. Reliable and honest credit counselors are accredited by the Council on Accreditation and do not charge ridiculous fees or make outlandish claims that they can "fix your credit report in 30 days," or "erase even the worst credit delinquencies." Most reputable credit counselors operate on a non-profit basis, and many are even offered through state or local governments.

Fixing credit takes time and commitment. If you encounter a credit counselor whose claims seem too good to be true, they probably are.

Imagine being 30 years old and still working to pay for the pair of shoes you bought during your sophomore year in college, or that tough chemistry class you decided to drop halfway through the semester. Sound crazy? Well, it's not: the average college student graduates with more than $20,000 of credit card and student loan debt. That means thousands of students will continue to pay for the decisions they made during college for years and years to come.

You don't have to join the ranks of students who are drowning in debt. While your circumstances may require you to accumulate some debt during your college years, if you manage this debt well, it will have a positive effect on your financial future.

This chapter will show you how by:

- Helping you understand debt.
- Recommending strategies to keep your debt under control and to pay off the debt you have.
- Outlining your options if your debt becomes overwhelming.

Understanding Debt

Student loan lender Sallie Mae conducts regular studies of college student spending and credit use that have revealed interesting – and alarming – information about students and debt. Recent studies have found that:

- 83% of undergraduate students have at least one credit card, a 24% increase since 1998.
- Students' average credit card balances are $2,327, a 15% decrease from the 2000 average.
- Students'median credit card balances are $1,770, a 43% increase above the median in 2000.
- 21% of undergraduates who have credit cards, have high-level balances between $3,000 and $7,000, a 61% increase over 2000 balances.
- Graduating students have an average of $20,402 in combined education loans and credit card balances.
- Students who reside in the Northeast use credit cards the least, while Midwesterners carry the highest average credit card balances.
- Students double their average credit card debt – and triple their number of credit cards – from the time they arrive on campus to graduation.

As these figures indicate, if you are a college student who is in debt, you are not alone. But don't be tricked into thinking that living with debt is just part of life. You can live your life free of overwhelming debt, but you must first:

Realize That Debt Can Be Positive

Accumulating debt and paying it off helps you establish good credit, which is important to everything from car insurance rates to the home you purchase. Accumulating debt for the right reasons can also aid your success – borrowing money to pay for an education that will help you succeed in your career, for example, or borrowing money to purchase a home that is a true investment in your future.

Understand Good Debt vs. Bad Debt

There are two types of debt: good and bad. What's the difference? Good debt is debt that returns something of long-term value to you, such as higher education. Bad debt can often be categorized as short-term "feel good" debt, like unwise purchases you can't afford and don't really need that are put on credit cards.

Know What An Acceptable Level Of Debt Is

Of course, ideally you would have no bad debt. But we all know that we live in a less than ideal world. However, the next-best thing is to keep your bad debt-to-income ratio lower than 15 percent. In other words, the total of your bad debt should equal no more than 15 percent of your annual income. If your ratio is higher, it should be a signal to you to get your debt under control as soon as possible. Generally, good debt should not be included in this ratio. However, if your home mortgage or student loan debts are staggering, you may wish to include those figures in your ratio.

Keeping Debt in Check

Managing your debt in a positive way is a constant process that involves a few important steps:

Know How Much Debt You Have
You can't keep your debt in check if you don't even know how much you owe. However, this is exactly the case with many college students and recent college graduates. If you spend the time to create a true picture of your debt, you may be unpleasantly surprised by the size and degree of your debt. Organize your debt in the following way:

Good Debt

Name of Loan	Principal Owed	Interest Rate	Annual Interest Payment (Est.)
Mortgage	$96,552	6.75%	$96,552 x 0.0675 = $6,517
Student Loan	$27,000	4.50%	$27,000 x 0.0450 = $1,215
TOTAL			

Bad Debt

Name of Loan	Principal Owed	Interest Rate	Annual Interest Payment (Est.)
Visa	$5,522	15.75%	$5,522 x 0.1575 = $870
Gas Card	$648	11.25%	$648 x 1.1125 = $73
TOTAL			

Know Your Debt Threshold
Familiarize yourself with the debt warning signs in the "What to do When Your Debt is Out of Control" section and take notice if you begin to approach any one of the warning signs. Set a debt limit and stick to it. When

you approach your threshold, take the necessary steps to control spending and reduce debt.

Pay It Off

Take a good look at your bad debt chart, focusing on the balance with the highest interest rate. Start by paying this off. Once you've paid off your most costly debt, don't stop there. Move on to the next one and pay that off. Work your way down the chart until you have eliminated all your bad debt. Here's how:

- ***Lose the credit cards.*** Freeze them in ice in your freezer or, even better, cut them up. Use only cash or a debit card so you can't spend what you don't have.
- ***Develop a budget.*** Study your spending habits, your obligations, and where you are most likely to get in trouble. Then develop a written budget that puts paying down your bad debt first, but also pays down your good debts on schedule.
- ***Live within your means.*** Stop all impulse buying and cut corners where you can. Pack your lunch, clean your own house, cancel cable television. Keep yourself motivated by continually reminding yourself that this is all about your future – maybe even your survival – in the real world.
- ***Pay more than the minimum due each month.*** Minimum payments are set by the bank to keep you paying interest forever. Pay as much as you think you can stand each month, and then add a few dollars to that.
- ***Transfer credit card debt to a low-interest card.*** If you have too much debt to transfer your lowest-rate card, pay the minimum due on all cards but the worst, and start making as large a monthly payment as you can on that one until you can roll all of your debt into one card. Any debts you can roll into a single debt at a lower interest rate will put money back in your pocket that you can then use to pay down the new, consolidated debt. But be sure to pay very close attention to the fine print involved with these cards, and familiarize yourself with the terms. Many Web sites offer information to help you compare various credit cards to get the best deal. Start with www.bankrate.com or www.cardtrak.com.
- ***Use your savings.*** As painful as it is, it makes no sense to let you savings sit there earning a piddling amount of interest (*which is taxable*) when you're paying a much higher interest rate on debt. Paying down your debt technically puts more money in your pocket in the form of interest you no longer have to pay, untaxed, than you can earn on most any savings account.
- ***Sell stuff you don't need.*** Have a yard sale or sell stuff on eBay. If you drive an expensive car, sell it and replace it with an economy model, or even go carless for a while and use public transportation.

- ***Get a part-time job.*** Use your spare time to make money you can put toward paying off your debt.
- ***Renegotiate with your lenders.*** Most lenders will work with you, particularly if your next choice is bankruptcy. Ask for forgiveness of fees, a lower interest rate, and/or a longer repayment schedule.

What to do When Your Debt is Out of Control

Take an honest look at the list below and decide if any of the statements describe you:

- ***Living from paycheck to paycheck*** with nothing left over at the end of each month.
- ***Impulse buying.*** Do you often buy things you don't really need or don't end up using?
- ***Making late or minimum monthly payments*** on your credit card(s), or skipping payments altogether.
- ***Having credit cards that are at, or close to, your credit limit.***
- ***Arguing with family members or friends over your spending habits.***
- ***Being unsure of how much you really owe.***
- ***Using cash advances to pay your bills.***
- ***Having more and more of your monthly income that must go to paying off your debts.***
- ***Having your credit card declined,*** or being turned down for additional credit.

If you recognize yourself in the above list, your debt may be out of control. Now what? You do have options. Here are a few:

Financial Advisors
Call your financial planner, if you have one. He or she can be an excellent source of advice. After all, part of their job is to discuss any financial problems you may have, and too much debt certainly qualifies.

Consumer Credit Counseling Service (CCCS)
If you want to renegotiate terms with your creditors, you can get free information from the non-profit Consumer Credit Counseling Service. Call (800) 388-2227 to find an office near you. They will give you general budgeting advice for free, and specific counseling for a low fee. Keep in mind, however, that using their programs may have a negative impact on your credit report, and they may not be able to recommend the solutions that fit your needs best. Beware, also, of unethical credit counseling services – there are plenty of them out there.

Collection Agencies

Although not a great option, one or more of your creditors may have turned a collection agency on you. Know your rights when it comes to collection agencies:

- ***A collection agency may contact you by phone, e-mail, fax, mail, or in person.***
- ***They cannot call before 8:00 a.m. or after 9:00 p.m.***
- ***They cannot call your boss or members of your family.***
- ***No one else can be forced to pay a debt that is yours alone.***
- ***You can get them to stop calling you by sending them a letter.*** They are then only allowed to contact you regarding plans to bring legal action against you.
- ***You do not need to tolerate rude or belittling remarks*** – but do not take that same attitude with the collection agency. After all, you do owe the money.
- ***Collection agencies are not empowered to work out terms of payment.*** They make money by collecting a percentage of the amount owed, so they will not cut deals on anything other than, perhaps, payment timetables.
- ***If you think you are being treated unfairly, contact the FTC*** at (877) FTC-HELP and ask for information on the Fair Debt Collection Practices Act, or visit the Web site at www.ftc.gov.

A Note on Bankruptcy

While bankruptcy is a drastic step that should only be used as a last resort, it is sometimes the only course of action left. There are two forms of personal bankruptcy – Chapter 7, which permits you to discharge certain debts, and Chapter 13, which gives you a debt repayment schedule. Chapter 13 does not discharge debts, but it does make creditors back off.

Drawbacks of bankruptcy:

- ***Bankruptcy will appear prominently on your credit reports for 10 years*** after you file for it. This means getting more credit will be difficult, particularly for the first few years.
- ***You are unlikely to be allowed to make a major purchase***, such as a home, in the first five to seven years following the filing.
- ***Filing for bankruptcy costs money.*** It will probably run you some $1,000, or even more, in filing and legal fees.
- ***Although there is a great emotional benefit to cleaning your slate and starting over, there is stress and some embarrassment that surrounds filing for bankruptcy***, including baring your personal affairs to court personnel,

lawyers and creditors, and having your personal finances placed under court control.

- ***Most likely you will not be allowed to keep expensive luxury items*** like jewelry, boats, multiple cars or other big-ticket items – they will be used to offset your discharged debt.

If it is your only option, there are some benefits to bankruptcy:

- ***Most likely, you won't lose everything.*** Most states allow you to protect a certain amount of home equity. In some states you may even be able to keep your home, no matter what it's worth, and you may be allowed to keep home furnishings, clothing, household goods, pensions and retirement accounts – so don't sell these off or empty out these accounts to pay off your debts unless you are certain you will never file for bankruptcy.
- ***Certain kinds of debts can be wiped away completely, or discharged,*** including:
    - Credit card debt
    - Auto loans
    - Rent payments
    - Medical bills
    - Utility bills
- ***Certain kinds of debt cannot be discharged,*** including:
    - Child support
    - Alimony
    - Taxes (both state and federal)
    - Court-ordered fines or damages

One bankruptcy experience should be enough for anyone. Get credit counseling and resolve to learn from your past mistakes. After bankruptcy is the time to start working toward a reasonable financial future and retirement.

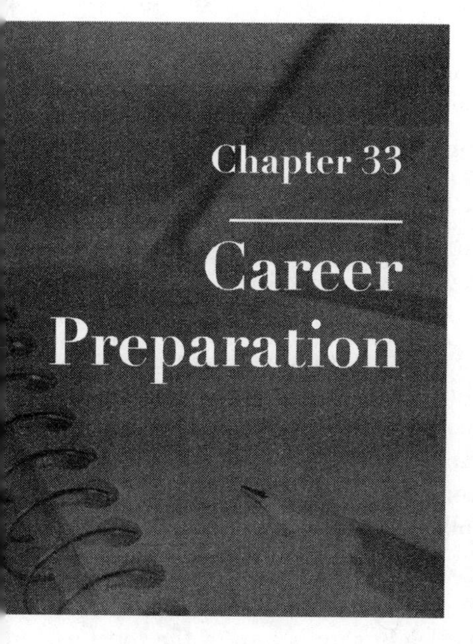

One of the biggest mistakes new college students make is focusing on college too much. It may sound crazy, but focusing solely on college is exactly what you don't want to do. In fact, this chapter will show that college students should focus on their future as much as they focus on their education.

The point of attending college is to prepare yourself for your future. That means developing yourself into a well-rounded person who is impressive to potential employers and equipped to meet and exceed the challenges of the real world. Achieving academic success and getting good grades is an important part of this development, but there are lots of other qualities, skills and experience you must acquire to be truly ready for your future.

This chapter will show you how to get ready for career success by:

- Outlining the kinds of skills important to career success and impressive to employers.
- Explaining the character strengths that appeal to employers.

Must-Have Skills

Of course, the specific skills you will need depend upon the career you choose. Reporters must know how to write, edit and craft a good story; computer programmers must know a variety of computer languages and how to use software and navigate networks. But there are a variety of skills that are valuable and necessary no matter which career path you choose.

Relevant Experience
A resume full of relevant work experience will be one of the first things to catch a potential employer's attention. Employers like to see that job candidates have challenged themselves with activities outside of their academics, and that they have been able to successfully apply the skills learned during college in a work setting. As discussed in the educational employment chapter, there are a variety of ways to gain valuable work experience while you are in college. Make sure you do!

Strong Communication Skills
Being able to listen, speak and write effectively are some of the most important skills for success. Your ability to communicate will come through in your cover letter and resume and during the interview process, but being able to further prove your communication skills with public speaking, debate or writing experience is even better.

Ability To Work Well With Others
No matter how impressive a candidate's skills, no matter how amazing their achievements and experience, if an individual is unable to work with others, he or she is virtually worthless to a potential employer. Effective teamwork is essential to the success of every company and organization, and employers want to see that a candidate is a good team player through evidence like membership in clubs or activities, successfully completed group projects, or awards and recognition from part-time jobs.

Leadership
Every employer wants to hire a leader. But leadership is one of the most difficult skills to identify and quantify. Management classes prove that you have the academic knowledge necessary for leadership, but hands-on experience proves that you have been able to apply what you have learned in the real world. Employers will be impressed by leadership roles you have taken in clubs, activities or employment.

Technological Know-How
In this day and age, employers don't simply hope that their employees are technology-savvy – they require it. Make sure you have the technological know-how you need by becoming experienced in the software programs used in your industry, and know how to navigate the Internet. Also be sure to expand your computer and technology knowledge whenever possible.

Flexibility
A job candidate who demonstrates the willingness and ability to adapt to change, respect for differences and diversity, and an interest in developing skills and experience outside of his or her comfort zone is very attractive to potential employers. A few ways to develop evidence of this skill are to complete coursework outside of your major, participate in a variety of

activities in diverse areas, including internships, part-time employment, volunteering and school activities, and by studying abroad or learning new languages.

Good Grades – And More

Of course, every potential employer loves to see a high grade point average. But your grade point average is only one way employers assess your value as a job candidate. Focusing all of your time and energy to achieve a perfect grade point average can actually be counterproductive. Developing a more well-rounded college career, complete with activities, leadership roles, relevant employment and a variety of enriching experiences – along with a respectable grade point average – is far more impressive than a perfect 4.0 and nothing else to show for four years of college. Of course, letting your academics suffer because you are over-extended and short on time isn't a good idea either. Achieving the perfect balance is the key – in college and in life.

Necessary Character

While employers will look at your education, experience and achievement, most employers admit that in the decision to hire a candidate or not, an individual's character is as important as all of these other items. What is character? Quite simply, it's the kind of person you are. Responsibility, loyalty, honesty, dependability, respect, creativity, resourcefulness, kindness – all of these are markers of good character.

It is difficult to demonstrate a strong character during the job interview process, but employers will look for clues to your character in your cover letter, on your resume, from your references, and from you. For example, you can show that you are dependable by indicating in your resume that you completed all of your coursework on time. Pointing out during your interview that you developed a new and better system of student government voting while serving on the student election board is a great way to prove your creativity. A comment from a reference about the time you stayed late to help finish a project on deadline the last day before your spring break will demonstrate your loyalty.

Be sure to emphasize these kinds of things in your cover letter and resume, include this kind of evidence on your resume, and choose your references well.

Shortly after graduation, many new college graduates find themselves in a classic Catch-22: they want to start a brilliant career with the job of their dreams, but find that to get their first job they must have work experience in their chosen field. It's true – even entry-level jobs often require that you be able to fill in the "relevant experience" portion of the application. But don't worry – there's something you can do to avoid getting caught in this conundrum. It's called educational employment.

Educational employment, very simply, is employment you pursue while still earning your college degree that furthers your education in the field of your choice. The most common kind of education employment is called an internship – but there are actually many different kinds of educational employment available to you, from part-time jobs and volunteering, to externships and work-study.

Many college students believe that educational employment isn't important until their junior or senior year – but this couldn't be farther from the truth. Getting a leg up on work experience, even in your earlier college years, is a great strategy.

This chapter will show you how to attain the best educational employment experiences possible by:

- Outlining the different types of educational employment available.
- Recommending ways to find educational employment opportunities.
- Giving tips on how to find the educational employment opportunities that fit you best.

Types of Educational Employment

Creating an impressive resume of well-rounded and relevant experience during your college years can take some outside-the-box thinking. While landing a prestigious internship at the same company you would like to land a job at once you graduate would be wonderful, it's not always possible. But you can still get some amazing in-the-field experience that will knock the socks of future potential employers by exploring all of the options available to you, like:

Internships

Internships are short-term employment assignments during which you receive valuable hands-on training and experience in a career field. Some internships last a college term, while others may be year long or take place during the summer break. Some colleges actually coordinate internships for students – placing students in an employment situation with a participating company or organization and awarding college credit for the internship work completed by the student. Usually you will have to pay tuition for this kind of internship, and may have to attend a college-planned seminar and/or complete a project at the end of the internship, such as a paper or presentation about your work experience. Other internships are not arranged with the help of your college, and instead are an agreement between the company and the student. Students do not receive any college credit for these kinds of internships and do not have to pay any tuition. Some internships like this are paid, while others are not.

Cooperative Education

If your college offers a cooperative education program, it can be an ideal way to develop your resume while earning your education. Cooperative education is very similar to internships, with a few key differences. With cooperative education, students usually are required to attend an academic class in conjunction with their job assignment. This class is designed to support the experience you are receiving through your employment, and will often include lessons about important employment issues like ethics and teamwork, and will help you develop the skills necessary to succeed in your chosen career. Cooperative education programs often last longer than just one college term – in fact, many cooperative education programs place students in employment situations for the duration of their education, and may even include monetary compensation.

Externship

Very simply, an externship is a mini-internship. During an externship you will spend a very brief period of time, perhaps a day or a week, following an employee of a business or organization through their workday. An externship is designed to give you a quick view of a career, and allows you to work alongside a person in the career of your choice, ask questions and advice, and perhaps complete a small task or project to give you an idea of the kinds of challenges you would face in this career. Because externships take place in a short period of time, many college students complete them over spring or summer break.

Volunteering

Many college students volunteer because they enjoy it or are committed to helping a worthy cause. But if opportunities are chosen well, volunteering can actually be a great way to receive valuable hands-on experience in the field of your choice. For example, if you are interested in a medical career, volunteering at a hospital or medical clinic is a smart choice. Want to work in education? Volunteering for an after-school program or tutoring at-risk kids can get you on the fast-track to career success. Is event planning your career goal? Volunteer with an organization and offer to plan events, charity drives and meetings.

Summer And Part-Time Jobs

Most college students work at some time during the year anyway, so why not make your part-time or summer job a stepping stone to career success? Even though spending your days at the beach as a lifeguard may be great fun, you would do better to choose employment that is relevant to your career path. For example, if you are interested in a career in law, try finding a job answering phones or working as a gopher for a local law firm. Think teaching is your thing? Working as a counselor at a youth camp would be a good choice. Considering a career in hotel or restaurant management? Working at a local inn or eatery is for you.

Work Study

You may be able to find valuable work experience without ever leaving campus. Many colleges offer work-study programs in which students work in order to subsidize tuition or other college expenses. Talk with your advisor or with your school's employment office to see if there are opportunities that would be relevant to your career choice. For example, if you are thinking about a career in science, perhaps there is a lab assistant position available in your college's science department. Human resource majors might find valuable experience working as a student assistant in the college's human resources or benefits department, while an agriculture major might be able to secure a job working with the college landscaping crew.

Finding Educational Employment Opportunities

You now know the importance of educational employment and understand the different kinds of educational employment available. Now, how do you go about finding the educational employment opportunity that meets your needs? First, start with your college career center, advisor or employment office. Your college offers a wealth of education opportunities, both on campus and with companies and organizations that have developed relationships with the college. However, opportunities sponsored and arranged by your college can be very competitive and hard to come by. Oftentimes, to find the perfect educational employment, you will have to secure the opportunity on your own. Here's how:

Get To Know Your Instructors
College instructors often have the best information about educational employment opportunities because they have established relationships with business owners and leaders in the community. Don't be afraid to ask your instructors if they know of any great opportunities that they would recommend.

Check The Alumni Center
Your college alumni center probably maintains a database of alumni with information about their employment. See if your alumni center will furnish you with a list of alumni who work in the career of your choice and would be willing to speak with you about opportunities or to give you recommendations or advice.

Look In The Yellow Pages And Make Calls
One of the easiest ways to get a line on educational employment opportunities is to look in the Yellow Pages for businesses and organizations that are relevant to your career choice. After finding out a little about these businesses, call their human resources or employment offices to see if there are any educational employment opportunities available – including internships, externships, part-time work and volunteer positions. Even if an opportunity is not currently available, ask for an appropriate contact and send him or her your resume – an opportunity may become available at a later date.

Check In With Professional And Trade Associations
Professional associations and clubs often help their member businesses and organizations find quality candidates for internships, volunteer positions and part-time work by listing opportunities on their Web site, in their newsletter, on a job board, or by spreading the news by word of mouth. Even if the association does not know of current opportunities, they may be able to give you a list of businesses that could have educational employment openings.

Eye The Internet
The Internet, of course, is a great resource for seeking education employment. Some of the big employment search engines now even list internships, part-time work and volunteer positions. You can also use the

Internet to gather information about potential educational employment opportunities.

Ask Friends And Family – And Networking Contacts
Don't forget networking when it comes to educational employment. Your friends, family and the contacts you have developed through networking can be invaluable when it comes to securing educational employment positions. Chances are, someone you know is connected to someone in the career of your choice – all it takes is for you to ask some questions.

Choose Wisely

If you are like most college students, you are very busy and have limited time for anything outside of academics. That's why it is essential that you choose the educational employment opportunities that will give you the most value for your time.

Before accepting an educational employment position, think it through and ask yourself a few key questions before making your decision:

- Will this position help me develop the skills and experience I will need to land the job I want after college?
- Have I read and do I understand the job description and expectations? Can I fulfill the requirements and meet the expectations?
- What kinds of projects will I be working on? What kinds of projects have past students worked on, and what have the results been?
- Have I spoken with other students who have worked with this company or organization? What was their opinion of their experience and this company?
- What kind of monetary compensation will I be receiving? If I am receiving no financial compensation, will I be receiving educational credit or work experience as valuable or more valuable than cash?
- What kinds of expenses will I incur with this opportunity? Is the position out of state, requiring me to pay for moving and housing costs? Do I have to take public transportation or spend a lot of money on gas to drive to this job? Do I have to buy a new wardrobe, new computer software, a cell phone or other accessories? If so, will my employer offer any kind of subsidy to help me pay for these expenses?